The Good Fight

GreatCommission**Society**
SEMPER FIDELIS, SEMPER PARATUS

The Good Fight

Vasile Tofan

Great Commission Society

Copyright © 2017 Vasile Tofan

Published by Great Commission Society
Suite 1, 4 Queen Street
Edinburgh
EH2 1JE
Scotland

DISCLAIMER
This book tells the true story of Vasile Tofan. Some scenes have
been dramatized with authentic though not necessarily actual
dialogue, and – to protect the author and his family, and the rights
of those whose paths he has crossed – some of the names, places, and
details of the events have been altered.

British Library Cataloguing in Publication Data
A catalogue record for this book is available from the
British Library

ISBN: 978-1-908154-31-6

Cover design by EKDESIGNS
Typeset by Avocet Typeset, Somerton, Somerset, TA11 6RT
Printed and bound by Nørhaven

THANKS

I give thanks first of all to my Lord Jesus Christ, for His grace and companionship, and to the Holy Spirit, for His inspiration and guidance throughout the process of writing this book.

Then I give thanks to my wife, Mirela, for her support in prayer during my effort to complete this work and – something that gives me great joy – because she is a godly wife.

I give hearty thanks to my beloved brother, Ioan Panican, a special man who means the world to me in my life of faith. If he hadn't been insistent and encouraged me many times as a special spiritual father, this book wouldn't have come to life.

I also give thanks to my friends and brothers in the faith with whom I attend the sessions at the Maranatha Bible School, who have encouraged me to finish this third edition of the book; being amazed, from the first time they heard my testimony, at the wonderful way in which the grace of God manifested itself in my life, changing it completely.

Among these, I had the privilege of meeting Teodor Pandrea – a beloved brother. I was very glad that this man, who is highly educated and of vast professional experience, considered me, a simple and unworthy man, one of his friends. I had many talks with him and

I was impressed with the warmth, love and friendship with which he addressed me. When I considered publishing this book again, I got in touch with him, asking if he could take care of this. I was deeply moved when I heard back from him that he was honoured to accomplish this sacred job. I know that, if he had been alive, he wouldn't have agreed to me writing this 'thank you' to him because of his humility. Today he is home with the Lord, and I pray that God would reward his hard work and bless and comfort all his dear ones, especially his sister Rodica, his wife, and his beloved children.

I also give thanks to my potential readers who are 'behind bars' (where I was once), wanting to be free, and those 'outside the bars' (who think they are free), and I pray that both categories mentioned here would thirst and hunger for the true freedom that only Jesus Christ can give. He said: '*You will know the truth and the truth shall set you free*' (John 8:32).

FOREWORD

Created in the image of God, man has, during his life on earth, numerous and various experiences, each one more interesting than the last. His destiny seems tragic and incomprehensible, rather than happy and majestic. Everything makes sense when man puts the sacrifice of our Lord Jesus Christ as the foundation of his life (past, present and future). Since the fall of Adam, who was the first of all mankind, people are born into the world as children of a prisoner, in a jail. From Adam we inherit not only the biological genes, but also the human destiny appointed by God. There we also find the roots of the common misery of mankind. Everyone's will has been perverted. Adam's sin and the atoning death of the Lord Jesus are not only the axis of the Bible; they are also the axis of the history of mankind. In Adam, we were all appointed to have a wretched fate, but in Jesus Christ, we all receive a new destiny.

In the same way, when you read this book carefully, documenting Vasile's testimony, you discover an old Vasile Tofan with a terrible destiny, and then a new Vasile Tofan with a happy and blessed destiny.

Man can be very wrong in analysing the behaviour of those around him, but at the same time he can be very wrong regarding himself. In the same way, those around us can be wrong about us. When we examine ourselves, we are both the examiners and the examinees, and we also decide the content of the exam. Vasile Tofan truly believed he was a good man. To lie is one thing; to believe the lie is totally different. He was sincere, but he believed a lie. It is not important what we say about ourselves, nor what others think and say, but ONLY WHAT GOD SAYS! *'For all have sinned and fallen short of the glory of God,'* as the Apostle Paul said in one of his letters. Vasile Tofan and I were among these people, and you, dear readers, like us, are also among these people.

The terrible problem of mankind is sin, which destroys the life of the individual, of the family, and therefore, by implication, of society too.

I Was Blind, But Now I See is an exciting testimony of the way in which our Good God met the author when he was in a time of despair. Is it necessary and mandatory that man collapses first, to realise the dead end he is in, so that later God can become necessary, real, alive, close, full of love, compassion, forgiveness and power? This is a question to which the answer is 'yes', in Vasile Tofan's case.

God is our Heavenly Father! Man's heart desperately needs peace, joy, comfort – in one word, it needs **salvation**. This cannot be achieved through education, training or religion – even if it is Christian religion. Much less can it be satisfied by money, relationships or good deeds. God's answer to the problem of sin is only one: THE CROSS OF CHRIST, as Vasile Tofan so clearly affirms when he says: 'He who believes in Jesus, in the blood that was shed on the cross at Golgotha, receives four great blessings: he is forgiven of all the sins he ever committed, his soul is saved, he becomes a child of God and he receives the gift of eternal life.'

Society rightly condemned Vasile Tofan for the felonies he committed. By faith, and with holy repentance, God forgives us and gives a new and infinite hope. At the right time appointed by Him, God revealed Himself to Vasile Tofan. Now he is a new man, useful to his family, church and society. His thinking is just, because his horizon – once very narrow and dark – has broadened and been enlightened. Saint Augustine once said: 'The empty hole in man's heart has the shape of God, and that is why it cannot be filled with something else, but with God Himself and only Him.' Vasile Tofan, like all other people, had this empty hole, into which God thought it right to 'come into being' through His Son, Jesus Christ.

This book, *I Was Blind, But Now I See*, calls us all to meditate seriously about making some immediate and firm and lasting decisions.

I congratulate the author, and I wish with all my heart for him to grow continually in spiritual things, in the inner man, through God's grace and power.

Ioan Panican
Bucharest, November 2011

Chapter 1

I was born on 19 November 1968 as the third child of Maria and Ioan Tofan, a family who came from Bacău (a county in Moldova, Romania) but who lived in Galati (a county further south). Probably my father had hoped to take home a little girl from the maternity hospital, taking into account he had two sons at home. I never asked him whether he rejoiced or not when the nurse told him he had a boy. My parents, simple people from the countryside, with some fear of God, decided to name me Vasile. I never asked them why they chose this name, but I assumed they wanted to have the name of a saint in their family (Saint Vasile is a Romanian Orthodox saint, celebrated on 1st January each year in Romania, and translated elsewhere as Basil), taking into account that my two other brothers were named Milica and Dan.

I remember how much I enjoyed going to a little village near Adjud, visiting my maternal grandmother, Ilinca. Every summer I saw my cousins, who came to spend their summer break at Ilinca's house. I really enjoyed taking the villagers' animals to the pasture in the village, even if my greatest problems were caused by my relatives' goats, which were very rebellious – and that really upset me!

What gave me the greatest pleasure was *miutza*

(something like a football game), which I played with the boys in the village. Every Sunday, all those around my age met on a central playground and played football until our knees were bruised. Despite many other experiences, it felt like summer break was soon over.

In school I was a 'middle platoon' (meaning average) student. I was not very diligent in learning, but I wasn't the last in my class either. I knew that if I made failing marks I would have had to deal with my father, and his belt, and I didn't want to experience such 'caressing'. In my class, because of my temperate behaviour, I was bullied by others who wanted to show off by taking advantage of boys like myself.

Milică, my older brother, who was six years older than me, used to come and protect me. But when I was in the sixth grade, Milică, who was annoyed at being my protector for so long, took me to the gym at the Oţelu boxing club. Here I was introduced to his coach, Ovidiu Enache, and my brother told him to 'do something' with me. The gym was in the courtyard of the Metallurgic High School No. 3. As I was very skinny at that time, I hid behind the punch bags, and I was afraid of the day when I was going to be the next one to have my nose broken. At least, this story was invented by those who were called 'seniors', to make fun of those of us who were just beginning. Seeing that I was rather withdrawn, the seniors arranged a sparring match for me with someone who was very experienced by comparison.

Unable to avoid the meeting or to postpone the fight, I found myself in the middle of the ring. I was overwhelmed with fear at the thought of the punches

I was about to receive, and so I placed myself on guard, and I started to loosen my arms on the 'line'. My advantage was the fact that I was taller by about 30cm than Sergiu, my opponent...and Sergiu stoically received all the punches I sent right to his face. At the end of three rounds, my first adversary had a completely bruised face from my punches! To the great surprise of those present, I was the winner. My victory that day made my coach, Enache, see in me a fine future boxer, and it gave me great motivation.

And so, from the nice well-behaved little boy of School No. 31, Micro 38 (a district of the city of Galați), I became the most feared boy in the school – and all that was due to the fact that I won the match in the gym of the Oțelu boxing club.

Even though I liked this position – the toughest boy in school – I gave up boxing *sine die* (with no set date for taking it up again).

Two years later, I met Ovidiu Enache again by accident in a tram station in a district close to mine. The man who had put boxing gloves into my hands for the first time had not forgotten me, and following a long conversation, he managed to persuade me to go back to the boxing ring.

Three months later, in the summer of 1985, I won the bronze medal at the National Boxing Championship after a disputed decision of the referee, who declared a boy from Medgidia as the winner. Even though I won just the bronze medal, I was selected to be in the National Junior League. Here I was the peer of two men who later became world champions, Francisc Vaștag and Mihai Leu. Our coaches, who were training us for the European and World Championships, were Calistrat Cuțov, Vasile Bala and Relu Auras.

I was an ambitious sportsman and I was making remarkable progress. Unfortunately, an incident that happened at a friendly boxing match in DRG (Democratic Republic of Germany – this was the communist part of Germany before the fall of the Berlin Wall) stopped my progress for about a year and a half. What happened there? Because some of my colleagues usually came back with their pockets full of good things from the German stores, I went out to 'take' a pair of jeans. I didn't know that the store had video cameras, and I was caught while I was taking the jeans. Following this incident, the staff of the Boxing Federation wanted to suspend me for life. Puiu Bădescu was the secretary of the Federation at that time, and he was very upset with me, but because I was a boxer with great potential, he gave me just an eighteen-month suspension.

I didn't quit boxing. I continued to train, and I boxed under a false name in the places where I was unknown. When my suspension ended, I won the 'Moldova's Belt' in Iasi in 1987, this time in the senior league. A year later, I had to enroll in the army, and I did my military service at the Olympic Centre in Târgu Jiu. When I finished my military service in November 1989, I continued with my sports career at the Gloria Club in Galati. In the summer of 1990 I transferred to the Dunarea Club, and after that I came back to the Oțelul Club, having Mr Ovidiu Enache again as a coach. In 1991, I competed at the National Boxing Championships in Bucharest, where I won the bronze medal. I made good progress; in the semifinals of the +91 kg category, I competed against Daniel Dăncuță, from Bacău, with whom I had trained for a few months at the Dinamo Club. Technically I was superior but his force gave him the victory. I was surprised by a terrible punch, and Daniel won with a KO (knock out). Thus I missed qualifying in the category finals.

After that I had a difficult time in my life because of a reorganisation at my workplace, the Galati Naval Mechanic Factory. In 1992, with the help of my Aunt Aglaia, who kept encouraging me, I enrolled in the gendarme force within the Internal Affairs Ministry. Here I was very encouraged by my superiors, at that time Major Lieutenant Ionel Florea and Colonel Lieutenant Vasile Harabagiu. Due to these two special men I was able to continue my sporting activity. I didn't fail them, and the same year, in 1992, I 'unofficially' became national champion. How did that happen?

In the final match, with super-heavy Vasile Damian, I was treated incredibly unfairly in the scoring. All the audience at the Floreasca ring saw just one winner – me – but the referees preferred my opponent, thus stealing the title that I so wanted. I had to come back to Galati as the vice-champion of Romania; I was so sorry I couldn't come home as the champion, even though I had made many and great sacrifices that year. Because our club in Galati didn't have the means to provide the right resources for me, I had spent a lot of money out of my own pocket as a gendarme. Laurențiu Gafițiuc, a good friend of mine at that time, helped me with the necessary medicines, food and other expenses. My coach was Stelian Lungu (nicknamed Samir), who was another friend of mine. The way in which my club 'rewarded' me, with just 15,000 lei – approximately fifty US dollars – for the vice-champion title, caused me to abandon the enthusiasm and rigour with which I had approached all my training. The next year, 1993, I only won the bronze medal at the National Championships, because I was totally unprepared physically.

From that moment on, a thought captured my mind and heart more and more, and that was to leave the country. I knew that if I had the right training I would be able to achieve great results in boxing, and so I started dreaming about the West. I knew of Mihai Leu, who had a career in Germany, and I was looking for a chance to get to a country that could provide the necessary resources for me to become a great champion. Boxing was, and still is, an extremely difficult sport, and if you don't have the right conditions you cannot have a brilliant career, such as I was dreaming of.

In 1991, during an international tournament in Spain, I met Valentin Silaghi, one of Romania's champions in the eighties. Because of the conditions, and probably because of the desire for a different life, the former champion had moved to Germany in 1982-1983. When I met him in Spain, he was there as the coach for Germany. After we talked, he gave me to understand that if I had a chance to get to Germany, he would help me.

From that moment on, I started to think how I could get there as soon as possible. Due to my financial situation I couldn't afford to leave right away, but I started hoping, dreaming, that an opportunity could arise somehow. Because I wanted to continue my sport activity, and because I also knew that excellence is not achieved without money, I looked for a sponsor. One day I met the owner of a restaurant in Galati, with whom I shared my plans and aspirations. At first, this man was interested and invested some money in the things that were needed for my physical training. I was now beginning to hope that my desire to be a great champion was about to come true.

After each training session I ate at this man's restaurant and then, one day, I met a friend of his who lived in France. Hearing about me from his friend, he had expressed the desire to meet me in person. After he'd listened to me, he showed an interest in investing in me, and offered to take me to Western Europe. When I heard his words, I couldn't believe my ears. Finally there was 'sunshine on my street' (a Romanian saying, meaning that things are finally getting better for you), especially since this man suggested I go to...Germany. It felt like it was a dream! I ran home to tell my wife Mirela, whom I had married in 1991, and I told her we were going to be the happiest of people.

I had met my beautiful wife at a high school in Galati. She was a student at Alexandru Ioan Cuza High School, a very fine school with an excellent reputation. When I first saw her, I fell in love with her, fascinated by her brown, piercing eyes and long, black hair. When her father found out that I was a professional boxer, he was against our friendship, saying that he didn't want any bullies arriving at his door. I was not impressed with his refusal, but I continued to fight for this beautiful girl to be my wife.

I forbade Mirela, who was my girlfriend at that time, to come watch me box, because I couldn't fight in the ring knowing that she was in the audience. After we got married, I found out that she had broken this arrangement once, when she came to Brăila to watch me fight in the Covaci Memorial, which I won because my opponent abandoned the fight.

In May 1988, I'd had to do my military service. It was quite hard to leave and be separated from the one I wanted to woo. I finished my military service, and Mirela graduated from high school. We were married in 1991, and the only one who gave us their blessing was Roxana, my mother-in-law. Mihai, my father-in-law, was still against it. We had a beautiful wedding in November of the same year, and the Ionescus were our godparents.

I had met Mr Ionescu at the high school where I studied. He was a fine man, a foreman at the workshops we had at school. He and his wife Sanda, a lady who liked us the very moment she saw us, agreed to be godparents for us. So, on 2 November 1991, we had our wedding at a hall in Galati, and Mirela became my wife.

We lived with her parents for a while, and then we moved to a rented apartment in Micro 19, a district in Galați. After only two years, our marriage was really struggling because I was absent a lot from home, spending time with other people I was hanging out with. My wife was not very pleased with how I treated her, but she couldn't do anything and so she just kept crying and going to work as a shop assistant in a food store. I loved her dearly, knowing that she was at home and nobody could take her away from me, but I was spending most of the time with my friends. As the days passed by, Mirela became sadder and sadder, and upset in her heart because of my behaviour. She cried so much, she began to regret the day we were married.

Chapter 2

In October 1993, along with the man who lived in France and a friend of his, I left for Germany. Before I left, I went to my workplace to discuss with my boss, Mr Florea, the terms of my resignation. I explained my desire to leave for Western Europe and Mr Florea didn't oppose my wishes, and agreed to me resigning.

I left for Germany daydreaming about the future. I was thinking that, finally, I had the opportunity to afford everything I wanted. I was fed up with the fact that the people I hung out with had lots of money – more than I could ever have or imagine. At that time I thought that happiness meant lots of money, a fancy car, a nice house – in one word, to enjoy life. I hadn't heard about eternal life; I had no clue what it was. In fact (like many others), I thought that life was just what we could have here on earth, which I wanted to spend in fun and parties, because there was no other life available to us. For me, God existed and was needed only when things were tough, and when I needed a solution to my problems. The greatest need I had, and with which I pleaded with God to help me, was when I was in the ring fighting; I would pray for victory over my opponents, so that I could win the matches. Most of the time I won the matches, and after I received the money in an envelope, I would forget about God and continued indulging in immoral pleasures – depravity, disco, nights spent in bars, and so on.

Easter celebrations made me think more about God. I was so impressed with all the multitudes that went to church on Easter Eve and participated in a Romanian Orthodox custom when people take 'light' from the church in the form of a lit candle. Unfortunately, I didn't know much about God, only what my parents had told me, and so I didn't know the significance of Jesus Christ's death and resurrection. In the house I grew up in there was no Bible, so I had no clue about what it said. I don't really remember how old I was when I saw my grandmother reading the Bible, but I wanted to take it from her hands and see what was inside a book that I knew to be considered 'holy'. When I tried to do that, my grandmother held on tight to the book, and threatened me with her finger, saying: 'Don't you dare touch this book, unless you are determined to read it from the first to the last page! If you don't do it this way, God will punish you!'

I thought I was too young to read this book from the first to the last page, but I was determined to read the Bible when I was older, because then I would have the time, and my desire to have fun would have passed away.

I was going to Germany, the country of my dreams, with great expectations of what lay ahead. The day I left, Mirela was crying in front of the apartment building where we lived, but I was concerned with only one thing – to make a name for myself and become someone important. That is why I was not impressed with her tears and still wanted to leave, in spite of the fact that she asked me not to. Mirela had become 'the woman who would wait for me at home'. I had started to lie to her excessively – sometimes I was sorry for what I was doing, but I had no power to stop. I was going ahead with the desire to become someone great

On our way to the 'promised land' we stopped at a restaurant to celebrate my future career as a pugilist. In the evening we took a room at a hotel in that town. The man who lived in France, whom I will name from now on as the Boss, came into my hotel room. After a few jokes, he became very solemn and told me he wanted to share something very serious with me. I was very attentive to what he wanted to share. And this is how I found out his real intentions for me and the real reason for our trip to Germany. It was not what he'd told me initially, and he was not at all interested in professional sport. He was a mobster who had left the country years before, and was now in the business of stealing jewellery from developed countries like Germany. I was perplexed by his words! Soon my dream to come back to Galați as a great champion was ruined. I was receiving a different offer: to become a professional delinquent, instead of the professional boxer I was dreaming of!

Because he saw how perplexed I was, he gave me until morning to think it over. If I then accepted his proposition, I was going further; if not, I would have to go back to Galati.

That night, I fell asleep very late. I had been raised in a family of simple but honest people, and the education I received at home had stopped me doing stupid things that would have meant having to deal with the police or the courts. So many thoughts were bombarding my mind. I was trying to calm down, but these thoughts would then come in different ways: 'What good is it if you are the best boxer in the country and yet don't have the money you desire?' or 'What good is it to have your name on the first pages of sports newspapers, and yet you cannot meet your needs and enjoy life?' After a tiring struggle, I eventually fell asleep.

The next morning the Boss came to my 'cell' to find out what my decision was. I said harshly: 'We are going all the way!' When he heard my answer, he grinned. He looked me in the eye and said that I was not going to be sorry, and that I would go back to Galați a rich man. Even though, in my heart, I wanted to go back to my beautiful wife, shame, self-pride and the desire to become rich didn't let me go back.

In the second half of October 1993, after many incidents trying to cross the border illegally, we got into Germany. We found lodgings quickly, with the help of an Italian friend whom the Boss had in Bremen.

For two weeks we walked the streets of this beautiful German city. The luxurious shops, and the alluring Western life, made me long even more to get rich; I was so impressed with the way of life that the Germans displayed! Sometimes I thought I was dreaming, and yet my eyes were open – and I was trying to convince myself that, if we succeeded with the Boss's plan, then my life would surely change for the better.

One day, the Boss took us to see the shop where we were going to do the robbery. We reached a beautifully lit display window, with shelves that had at least nine golden Rolexes and numerous bracelets, chains and rings, all of pure gold. All these captured not only one's eyes, but the mind as well!

We settled on the day of the robbery and on a plan – we were going to steal everything from the display window of this store filled with very, very expensive and luxurious jewellery. But after making our evil plan, I was overwhelmed with thoughts and worry regarding the robbery and the risks involved in case we failed in our attempt.

However, it was too late to go back! My pride was at stake; I didn't want to go back to Galați a 'ragamuffin'. All the people in my city, on the Danube, knew that I had left to fight as a boxer in the West, and that I would surely come back a rich person. So any hesitation disappeared from my mind, and I went on with the plan...

Chapter 3

Once we had our goal established, we decided to carry out our plan on 1st November 1993 and, together with a colleague, I broke the display window of the fancy Bremen jewellery shop.

According to our plan, I was going to break the window. I was instructed to hit it hard, because the window was not an ordinary one; it was armoured. When my colleague signaled, we pulled the hoods over our faces, and I started to hit it hard with a 10-pound sledgehammer. After about 10 blows, using my strength as a heavy-category boxing champion, I managed to make a fist-sized hole in the window. My colleague tried to get his hand through to pick up the jewelry, but he couldn't, so he used a plastic claw with which he 'cleared' almost everything that was on the shelves. After approximately two minutes, we ran towards a car that was parked nearby, in a place that was not very exposed to the public.

The robbery was a total success, due partly to the fact that, some time before, our Boss had tested how vigilant the policemen were. He had timed them to see how long it took them to arrive at the site.

One day, clothed in a suit and tie, and with a bouquet in his hand, the Boss had hit the display window hard, and the alarm went off automatically. The policemen from the nearest department came in two minutes and thirty seconds. When he'd instructed us, the Boss hadn't forgotten to tell us this very important detail.

Two hours after the robbery, we were gathered in our Boss's apartment, rejoicing and admiring the huge quantity of gold we had stolen. When he saw the gold, the Boss smiled and asked me: 'How many years would it have been necessary for you to work to make the money you made tonight in just two minutes?!' I was confused with everything that was going on and, even though I was not used to alcohol, that night I drank a few glasses of whisky to try to calm down.

I went to the apartment the Boss had rented for me, and I started dreaming. The web of pleasures and money was starting to entangle me. I could see myself in a fancy car, driving through my hometown. I began to think that it wasn't such a terrible mistake. I hadn't killed anyone, and I was thinking that my wife's tears would soon turn into tears of joy. The dreams were also stimulated by the few glasses of whisky that I had drunk…and so I slept like a log.

The next day, the Boss left for France to get rid of the 'merchandise' that we had stolen from the shop the night before. When he left, the Boss instructed us to keep a low profile while he was gone so that the German police would not check on us. We had crossed the border illegally, and we had no visa to stay in Germany. So we took heed of the Boss's instructions, and spent a few days with his friend in the apartment he had rented for us. After three days, the Boss came back with the money made from selling the jewellery in France.

The 1,500 DM (Deutsche Marks), my share, was an incredible amount of money for someone from Romania at that time. I ran to the post office, where the Italian, the Boss's friend, sent 1,000 DM to Mirela in her name. I called her and told her not to worry, assuring her that I would come back home a rich man. When she asked me how I had made the money, I lied to her, telling her that a boxing club had hired me. I couldn't tell her what I had been through and how I had really made the money.

A few days went by, and I tasted the pleasures and charms of the West. I was completely astonished with what I saw and encountered, and the desire to become a man who could afford any pleasure in life grew more and more every day. So many thoughts were going through my mind. I had vivid memories of the toil and effort in any gym where people box. What was my benefit from all these years of boxing? Almost nothing!

When we broke into the shop, I hadn't had to work too hard. And what was the benefit? A large amount of money, and the satisfaction of many pleasures. At that time, I thought that true happiness meant money and, consequently, all the things money could buy.

Later, I came to understand that this was all vanity, like Solomon said in Ecclesiastes: *'I said to myself, "Come now, I will test you with pleasure to find out what is good." But that also proved to be meaningless. [...]"Laughter," I said, "is madness. And what does pleasure accomplish?" [...]Yet when I surveyed all that my hands had done and what I had toiled to achieve, everything was meaningless, a chasing after the wind; nothing was gained under the sun.'* (Ecclesiastes 2:1-2, 11)

Because it was a perfect robbery, I fell asleep that night very happy!

The next morning, when I woke up, something in my heart shouted loud and clear that I was on a wrong path. An incredible anxiety filled my soul. I was trying in vain to cast out the thoughts that flooded my mind, but they kept coming back, over and over again. A tormenting question bothered me almost all the time: 'Am I still a man?'

Two weeks later, the Boss planned another robbery. This time it was going to be in a different city, 200-300 km away from Bremen. This city was Wolfsburg, and the store we were going to break into was in the shape of the letter 'U' upside down. It had a display window where there were gold watches, and another display window with gold jewellery.

After about two weeks of fun and enjoyment, the Boss summoned us to instruct us about the next hit. This time, my job was slightly different. Because we were aiming at two display windows, I had to smash the one with the gold jewellery, and my colleague was supposed to smash the display window with the gold watches.

Before we left for Wolfsburg to fulfil the plan, I phoned my wife. I asked her to keep her fingers crossed for me, because I told her I was going to have a difficult match that night. I assured her that I was going to win, because 'good' money was involved. I told her not to panic, because the next day I was going to phone her to tell her about the money.

At that moment, I didn't realise that I wasn't going to call Mirela for nine months!

At dusk, we drove in two cars to Wolfsburg, so that we weren't conspicuous. The Italian and I were in an Opel, and the other man who was going to be a part of the robbery was in the other car, with the man who had orchestrated the whole plan.

I was very restless that evening. In my heart I didn't like being in that place, and I would have loved to have been at home with Mirela, my heart's desire. I missed her so dearly.

Chapter 4

My mind was filled with all kinds of thoughts.

In the blink of an eye, we reached the place where we were about to go ahead with the plan. I took the hood and the 10-pound sledgehammer and went to the shop that had been indicated to us in a previous trip, which I was going to break into. After breaking the window, I was going to quickly hide in the boot of the car that had brought me there. This was the plan.

The Italian and my Boss left. My colleague and I reached the shop, pulled the hoods over our faces, and started to hit the windows hard. After 10-12 blows, with all my power, I was surprised to see that the window would not break, not even one single crack in it! I wanted to leave the sledgehammer and quit, but when I looked up, I saw the window had loosened in its frame. So I hit the upper part with more blows, and eventually I managed to get into the shop with half of my body. I took everything that was on the shelves – approximately 1.5kg of gold jewellery.

When I looked to see what my colleague was doing, I saw a German police car very close to us. I ran as fast as I could. Suddenly I heard a gunshot, which scared me terribly. I reached the car that had brought us there, and I hid in the boot. Both my colleague and I had to hide in the boots of the cars that had brought us, because the Italian and the Boss had valid papers, and so there was no risk if the police would have stopped them. And there was very little risk of them being stopped by the police, because the German force didn't stop cars with just the driver in them. And there was an even smaller chance they would search these cars. The idea with the boot was a very good one.

I could sense an unusual quietness around me. I was scared, and many thoughts bombarded my mind. I was thinking of my colleague who had been with me; I didn't know if he had managed to escape or not. Being in such a predicament, my next thought was to say a prayer, in which I pleaded with God not to let the German police get me. I was still in the trunk of the Opel, overwhelmed with many fears, reproaching myself for getting into such a terrible situation. Almost an hour had passed since I had got in there. Suddenly, I heard many voices and car noises. The voices got closer and closer, until they stopped near my car. I was almost breathless. I heard someone trying to open the car, and I could see the steering wheel from an opening in the back seat. A policeman opened the driver's door, and, with a torch, he started searching the car. My heart was as small as a flea, and I was watching his every move. Suddenly, he turned to the back seat and lowered it abruptly. I'm sure he didn't expect to find me there in the boot! I was 1.93m tall, and I weighed over 100kg. He made a loud noise and hurried out of the car. At that moment, I realised that my hope of getting away with it was practically zero.

I decided to get out of the car on my own. When I got out, the policemen surrounded me. They put me face-down on the ground and cuffed my hands. After they pulled me up, they searched me and found all the jewellery I had stolen, which I had placed in two pockets. It was the first time in my life I had ever been treated this way! I was living through some unbelievable moments that I'd never thought I would have. They put me in a police car, which drove quickly to the local police department. From what I could understand, the policemen were talking over the radio with their colleagues about the capture.

When I reached the police department, the people there were trying to communicate with me, but that was very hard as I couldn't speak a word of German. They decided to send me to a cell, after they took almost all of my clothes. I think it was almost midnight, and I had so many thoughts racing through my mind. It was hard to believe I was in a cell, arrested by the German police, in Wolfsburg. That night, in that place, my thoughts were all about my wife Mirela, whom I had promised to call the next day, to tell her about the outcome of the 'match' – about which I had lied to her! For the first time in my life, I was in a cell, arrested. Why was I there? It was because of my crazy desire to become someone, to get rich, and to become famous. Later, I was going to find a wonderful and true book, which, if people would believe and obey it, would lead to a truly happy and fulfilled life. The following words from this book fitted my situation: *'Those who want to get rich fall into temptation and a trap and into many foolish and harmful desires that plunge people into ruin and destruction. For the love of money is a root of all kinds of evil. Some people, eager for money, have wandered from the faith and pierced themselves with many griefs* (1Timothy 6:9-10).'

I was so tired physically and mentally, but in spite of all these things, later that night I fell asleep.

Chapter 5

It was very early in the morning when I heard several voices near my cell. Suddenly, I saw someone watching me through the peephole of the cell door. Maybe they wanted to make sure everything was okay before they opened the door? After some time, the door opened, and the person who came in signaled me to follow him. I was taken to a room where they took my fingerprints, and I was photographed from several angles.

After that, other policemen took me to a different building where I was cuffed with my left hand to a chair. In this office, there was only one man who wasn't wearing a uniform, and he asked me, in perfect Romanian, what I had done. Then another man came in, along with a lady, also dressed as a civilian, who was going to transcribe the interrogation. I assumed the investigation had begun. The man who was translating for me – I found out later – was a Romanian who had lived in Germany for many years.

They interrogated me for a long time, with some breaks. They were trying to find out as much as possible about me and how I had ended up committing the felony. At the end of the interrogation two policemen in civilian dress came in – and they had guns. They signaled me to follow them, and I was taken to the office of a prosecutor, who bluntly told me my next stop: Braunschweig Penitentiary!

In the evening, after a long car drive, I entered the gate of the penitentiary. The two policemen uncuffed me and handed me over to the guards, who were going to take me to a cell. I was taken to one of the sections of this penitentiary and into a cell with six beds. The first prisoner from that cell who greeted me was a Romanian-speaking man from the Republic of Moldova. The first question I asked him was: 'Can one escape from this place?' The Moldavian smiled, and told me to get up and look out the window. And so I did. I could easily see that not even a bird could get in or out of that place...and so I gave up that idea!

Because the cell door hadn't been locked, I went out into the hallway. The Moldavian told me that there were no Romanians among the prisoners in the hallway; they were just Germans, Russians, Africans, Arabs, Turks and Poles.

A few minutes after my 'installation', they brought me some food – but I didn't touch it. Then, shortly after that, we were told to get into our cells, because the cell doors were closed overnight. I went in and lay down on the bed, but it was so difficult for me to fall asleep. My thoughts immediately turned to my darling wife, who was waiting for my phone call and news of the 'match'. There was a real battle going on in my mind, and so much restlessness in my thoughts, but eventually I fell asleep.

The next morning, I woke up confused and depressed; there was so much grief and bitterness in my heart. I was far away from my home country, from my family and from the woman I had married, and whom I dearly loved. They brought food again, but I had no interest in it. For three days in a row I refused to touch the food that was brought to me. The people in the Education Department were informed about my refusal, and I was gently taken to one of their offices.

Because I couldn't speak German, another Romanian prisoner from a different section was brought in. He could speak German quite well. They asked me the reason for not eating for three days in a row, and I answered that I was so upset that I didn't want to hear about food, let alone eat it.

The Romanian who interpreted for me suggested that I ask to be taken to his section, because there were several Romanians there; and maybe, being with folks that I could talk to, my state of mind would change. I decided to take his advice, and after about an hour, I was moved to the new section.

Truly, there were more Romanians here – but I was taken to a cell with a Pole!

In the evening, in the rec room of that section, I had to answer many questions put to me by the Romanians there. I was so amazed to see the indifference of some of them to being locked up; they were cheerful, made jokes, and watched TV. Some of the Romanian prisoners recognised my name, especially because many of them were from Bacău, and they were knowledgeable about boxing; and they knew that, in 1991, I had fought against Daniel Dăncuţă from Bacau. At 9pm, after three hours spent with them, the lights were switched off, and each of us had to go to our cells until the next morning, when we met again for our walk in the prison yard. When I entered the cell and lay on my bed, my thoughts were all about my beautiful wife. I had no way to get in touch with her, and I just wanted to tell her that I was healthy, and that nothing bad had happened to me. The fact that I couldn't get this message to her bothered me terribly.

Then I thought about my parents, who also had no clue where I was. What would they have said about me, knowing that I was in prison? I was deeply regretting the offer of that man who had brought me to Germany for a totally different reason than the initial one! How much I desired to be with my dear ones! I was tormented with grief, but there was nothing I could do! I was now in prison, and I kept thinking about the time I had to spend there.

When the German policemen had brought me to the penitentiary, 'as a sign of encouragement', they said I was going to spend ten years there! I refused to think that I had to be locked away for so many years, but I was also thinking that, if the policemen had told the truth, then my life was finished. My marriage, my sport career, my life itself, was going to shatter. I was thinking I could have very well stayed at home, even if I couldn't afford everything I wanted; I'd had enough to eat and I wasn't that poor.

My thoughts were interrupted by the noise of the door cell opening abruptly. A guard came in and said my name, and I was taken to a room where two policemen and a translator came to interrogate me. First, they asked me about the robbery on 1st November 1993, the first one I had committed. I hesitated for a moment, and I raised my shoulders, meaning that I didn't know what that was all about. Then one of the policemen showed me the picture of the Boss. Maybe I was startled when I saw it, which could be easily seen on my face, and this was noticed by the policeman that was standing. At first I denied knowing this fellow, but the policeman who was interrogating me told me that he was sure I knew him. He then said that if I didn't admit this, my years of detention would multiply.

The policeman also told me that they had asked about me in Romania, and that my criminal record was 'clean', which meant I was not a convicted criminal with a criminal record. They knew I was just a victim of the real thief, the man who had recruited me. The fact that I hadn't committed any other felonies in Germany was also in my favour. Fear, and the desire to get back to Romania as soon as possible, made me admit the felonies, and I co-operated with my investigators.

Finally, exhausted by everything that had happened there, I admitted that the Bremen robbery was also committed by myself and my colleague. The policemen left happy with the way in which they had investigated me, and all they had learnt from me. I went back to my cell with the hope that my sincerity, and the fact that I had admitted to the robbery in Bremen, would be mitigating circumstances, and would help me get out of prison sooner.

In the evening, at 6pm, the prison guard took us to watch TV and interact with one another. To my surprise it proved true that, in that section, there were more Romanians than Germans, or any other nationality. They had all come to Germany with the same desire, to steal and make good money, and thus get rich quickly. Most of them were acquainted with detention because they had 'visited' the prisons in Romania, and they were not stressed at all; they didn't seem affected by the fact that they had no freedom. They were joking, and made plans for the future when they would be released from prison. I realised that, for most of them, crime was a way of life, something they were familiar with.

However, there was a young boy in that group, Gigi, whose behaviour was different. He was not like the other Romanians. He was from Suceava, Gura Humorului. A few days after I was taken to this section, I asked the guards to move me to this young man's cell, and after I got there, I had plenty of time to chat with this man. Truly, Gigi had a very civilised, quiet and balanced attitude. In a short time, we became the best of friends and we encouraged each other, hoping that finally all would end well.

Three months passed. I learnt during this time that living well in such a place depended mostly on the way you learned to communicate and come to terms with, and so understand, the reality there.

I celebrated the New Year of 1993-4 in the cell with Gigi. There was great pain in my soul, because I was so far from the person I loved so dearly, and whom I thought of so often – my darling wife! I was thinking also of the others in my family, but missing her was the greatest ache in my heart. I had no idea whether Mirela had found out about my arrest or not, and I was wondering how she was spending that special moment of the year. My hope to see her again, and continue my life with her, faded every day; I didn't know how long I was going to be in prison, and what sentence I would receive for what I had done. Time was running so slowly for me!

The Romanians who had been through detention before told me that only after six to seven months did they judge you and give you a sentence. Others comforted me by telling me that, after a year, it was possible to be set free. I couldn't get used to the idea that I had to be imprisoned for a year or more, and the regret over the two robberies was not helping me at all. My crazy desire to make money, to be someone, and to live life to excess, had largely brought me to this sad situation. The words of my mother were ringing like a church bell in my head: 'Better poor and clean, than with riches and terrible headaches!'

My mum was so right, and I hadn't listened to her words. I remembered all the good things my parents had taught me, and how I hadn't heeded them. How much I now regretted not listening to them! The pain in my soul was unbearable. My parents had given me good advice but, unfortunately, they couldn't give me the power to keep their advice!

In this penitentiary, I realised how precious freedom was. You can have all that you want, but if someone takes your freedom, it takes away your will to live.

In this prison, no matter how strange it may seem to the Romanian reader, we were very well treated. The food was very good, the guards were really civilised in the way they treated us, they spoke nicely and behaved kindly towards us; we had a modern gym, showers, a football field – in one word, all the necessary amenities. Yet, in spite of all of these, we lacked FREEDOM!

Freedom has such a big price, because God created

man to live freely; but because man doesn't know, or doesn't understand, the plan of God regarding himself, he loses his freedom to the prison of sin, vices and bondage that he lives with. Jesus Christ came to our world so that man could be 'born again' and regain his identity, the identity that he lost in the Garden of Eden. That is why the lack of freedom was the hardest thing to bear!

I wanted so desperately to phone home to hear my wife's voice. Unfortunately for me, I didn't have this right because I hadn't been convicted yet. If I wanted to phone home, I had to hire a professional translator who would translate my conversation to the guards. I didn't have the money to do that, and I didn't want to talk with the supervision of a translator.

Today, because God had mercy on me, the One who changed the course of my existence forever, I understand so well what I read in the Bible – the revealed Word of God – in Genesis 2:24 where it says: *'That is why a man leaves his father and mother and is united to his wife, and they become one flesh.'*

Thais is why I missed my wife so much, the one with whom I had become one flesh! Yet, when I was at home with Mirela, this perspective had never occurred to me. In fact, in the two years we had been married, I had been so mean to her! I had missed nights at home, so often spending this time with my friends from the gendarme department. I had lied to her so often about spending nights at work, and I was motivated by deceiving and harmful pleasures. At that time, I thought this was how real men had to behave, to show their wives they were not under their supremacy.

One day, I tried to phone Mirela, but the guards showed me two letters that they had received from the DA, letters that said it was forbidden for me to call Romania until the trial was finished and I had received the sentence.

It had already been three to four months, and I'd had no news from home, and all sorts of questions were going through my mind to which I had no answer. Would my wife wait for me until I had finished this sentence, which hadn't, as yet, even been pronounced? Would she file the papers for divorce and marry another man? How badly I had treated her, and how blind I had been! The fact that I had no answer to these questions, and to many other questions too, made me despair terribly. Who could save me from the abyss I was plunging into deeper every day?

Chapter 6

One day, one of the Romanians, who was going to be expelled from Germany, came and gave me a book. I was there with my cellmate as the Romanian told me that he had found that book in the penitentiary library. The book he was holding in his hands was the Bible! He told us he didn't understand a lot of it, but that I was the first now to take it from his hands.

I went to my cell determined to read from it. Suddenly my thoughts turned to God, the only One, I was hoping, who could save me from this terrible situation in which I found myself. I didn't know much about God, and I only went to church on special occasions or, of course, when I had a match and a lot was at stake. I considered myself a Christian, even though, to be honest, I had no clue what that meant.

The moment I tried to open the Scriptures, which I hadn't held in my hands before, something strange happened. A thought came through my mind, and I remembered what had happened a long time ago, when my grandmother had told me that I should read the Bible from the first to the last page. I was afraid that God would punish me if I didn't read it like that, so I opened the Bible at the first page, where it said *Genesis*. I managed to read all the 50 chapters, and I was deeply touched by a little story in chapter 37. A ray of hope came into my heart when I read about the way God dealt with Joseph. I was thinking that, if I went on to read the whole Bible, God would deliver me from prison like he delivered Joseph.

I moved on to the second book of the Bible, Exodus. I read this book, and I realised that things got really complicated. The next books, Leviticus and Numbers, painted the image of a vengeful, unfair God, who only loved one people – the Israelites.

What shocked me even more was the fact that God was destroying many nations through His people. Men, women, children, old people, animals, and so on were all put to the sword at His command. This confused me, and made me ask questions regarding the authenticity of the book I was reading. The image of God described in the books of the Bible I had just read was one that I couldn't get along with very well. In my mind, in my imagination, I was seeing the picture of an unfair, biased and vengeful God. I refused to read any further.

Exodus, Leviticus and Numbers totally threw me into a confused state of mind, so I left the Bible on the table and stopped reading it. I didn't know how to pray either, and I didn't have a prayer book, so the words I would say in my prayers were these: 'Lord, please get me out of this prison, and please help me to get back to my wife!'

Together with Gigi, I decided to fast every Wednesday and Friday. This meant no food and no drink until midnight. Every Wednesday and Friday it was so hard for us to have food on the table, and yet not eat it until midnight. I knew, from my mother, that if we fasted Wednesdays and Fridays, God would listen to us and answer our prayers; and yet neither my cellmate nor I knew what fasting really meant, or what the purpose of it was.

On Thursdays, all the cell doors were opened for an hour, and we could go for a shower, change the sheets on the beds, clean the cells and so on. There was a Romanian who was in the cell next to ours, on the right side of the hallway. He had just been arrested, and when I looked at his face, I saw something unusual and out of place for here. This man's face was filled with light, compared to our faces, where one could see stubbornness, rebellion and restlessness.

I asked my cellmate if he knew something about this Romanian. He said that the only thing he knew was that he came from Târgoviște, and that he had just been arrested. Then the hour in which our cell doors were open was finished, and the doors were locked again. In fact, the doors were locked for 23 hours out of 24 every day.

One day, my cellmate wanted to talk to this Romanian when we were in the prison courtyard. When we got back to our cells from this walk, Gigi told me that this man had a book in his hands that he read all the time. When asked, he said that it was the Bible he was reading from. His name was also Gigi. My cellmate commented that this Romanian seemed strange and, more than that, he told me that he spoke with him about God. Well, when I heard this, I expressed my desire to talk to this man too, and to get to know him better.

The next day, I approached him and I asked the usual question you ask in a prison: Why are you here? What did you do? When he answered, I thought he was a total liar. He said he didn't know why he had been arrested, because he hadn't done anything wrong. It was hard for me to believe that you can be arrested in Germany, and put in prison, without doing anything wrong!

This man's name was Gheorghe Sabău, and we started calling him 'Uncle Gigi'.

Even though I was sure in my heart that he had lied to me, I could easily see that Uncle Gigi was different to us, the rest of the prisoners, who were in that section. His face revealed something that couldn't be seen in our faces. His speech and his behaviour were different to ours. I also noticed that Uncle Gigi didn't use swear words, like the rest of us, including myself.

Uncle Gigi shared about God with me. He told me he was a Christian, and that he loved God. He started sharing from the Bible, the book he read every day. Suddenly, I remembered the Bible I had abandoned in my cell, and which I didn't want to read anymore. Uncle Gigi asked to see the book I had told him about, that I couldn't read, thinking that it couldn't have been a true Bible.

The moment I brought him the book, he opened it, looked through it, and assured me it was a real Bible – it was just that I hadn't started where I should have started. He explained to me that you should start reading the New Testament of the Bible first, and then the Old Testament. He turned a few pages and showed me, with capital letters, THE NEW TESTAMENT OF OUR LORD JESUS CHRIST. On the next page, he showed me a title: The Gospel of Matthew. He advised I start reading this book.

If I had had something else to do, I wouldn't have

started to read this book again, but I had nothing else to do for 23 hours out of 24, so I started reading the Gospel of Matthew. The next day, I continued reading the Gospels of Mark, Luke and John. Day after day, verse after verse, what I was reading in that book touched my heart, it made sense, and it interested me more and more. The image of a vengeful, unfair God, which was ingrained in my mind from reading the Old Testament, was replaced now with the image of a merciful, good God, who forgives and loves people so much that He came down from heaven in the Person of His Son, Jesus Christ, to seek and to save that which was lost.

I couldn't believe what was happening to me. The words of the four writers of the Gospels had penetrated so deeply into my heart! They attracted me like a magnet, and I was, therefore, spending hours reading the New Testament. I didn't want to go out in the courtyard for walks, or even to the rec room. What I really wanted to do was to read from this book, a book that fascinated me, day after day, because I was so impressed with everything I read! Every time I reached the story of Jesus' crucifixion I wept, as if I were a part of what was going on. Everything I read had a huge impact on me! I had never read something like this before, and I couldn't begin to imagine that all I was reading had actually happened here on earth. Every time I saw Uncle Gigi we would talk extensively about what I was reading, and I would ask him many questions. I was amazed that he had answers for every question I asked and, moreover, I was amazed by the fact that this man knew the Bible so well that all the answers he gave me were also from the Bible.

From my daily discussions with Uncle Gigi I found out about man's sin of disobedience, and how man became separated from God. Because he listened to the words of the devil, the man that God had created and put in the Garden of Eden was separated from God, and died spiritually (the expulsion of man from the Garden, told in Genesis 3). Furthermore, in the Epistle that Paul wrote to the Romans, in chapter 3 verse 23, it says: *'All have sinned and fall short of the glory of God.'* In the same letter, the Apostle Paul writes to the Romans that *'the wages of sin is death'* (Romans 6:23). But in His great love, God made a plan to save the whole of mankind: the sacrifice of Jesus on the cross at Golgotha.

The gospel (which means Good News) speaks to us of God's decision to forgive every sinner who trusts wholeheartedly in His Son. We can all be forgiven of our sins, if we believe that Jesus died in our place. To believe in Jesus means to read the Bible, to agree with it, and to accept everything that is written there; but to also **fulfil** what the Holy Scriptures say.

Chapter 7

As time passed by, my talks with Uncle Gigi Sabău were so pleasant and interesting. He was such refreshing company. Whenever I talked with the other Romanians I got bored very easily, because of the nonsense they were saying and also because of their lies, but Uncle Gigi spoke differently, and his words gave me peace in my heart that I hadn't experienced before. This made me desire to be more and more in Uncle Gigi's presence, and to spend less time with the other Romanians. I enjoyed listening to him very much and, when I would go to my cell, I would dive into the Book I loved so well. I kept reading it over and over again, and it was as if I had found a spring of clean, fresh water; I drank more and more, because it made me thirstier and thirstier. When I read John 3:16, I understood the essence of the death and resurrection of the Lord Jesus Christ. God sent His only begotten Son into our world, so that through His death and resurrection, man can be delivered from the bondage of sin and death and can have eternal life through Jesus Christ.

What a pity that most people don't read the Bible, and don't know what it says. In Romans 10:17 it says so clearly: 'Consequently, faith comes from hearing the message, and the message is heard through the word about Christ.' How important it is that every man should read the

Bible. The gospels I was reading became a mirror that showed me my true self.

Until I got to that penitentiary, I thought I wasn't that sinful, because I hadn't killed anybody. But when I read what Jesus Christ said in one of the Gospels – that even if you look at a woman lustfully, you have already committed adultery or fornication in your heart – I realised just how frightening sin was! If you committed it just in your mind, you had sinned; I now understood sin was much more than just the physical act.

I remembered, and pondered, how many times I had said about different people: 'I would kill this one!' or 'I would hit this one over the head!'...which meant I was already a murderer! Why hadn't I seen myself like I truly was? It was because I had never looked in the 'mirror', that is, the Bible, the Word of God, that shows you exactly as you are. I compared myself to other people, and when you compare yourself with others, you almost always 'look' better, because you have the tendency to see yourself as being better, more handsome and greater than others. However, sin is inside, in the heart! If every man would look carefully, and intently, in God's 'mirror' (the Bible) he would see himself as he really is: poor, blind and empty. And so it was, for the first time, I fully realised I was a sinner, deserving God's punishment. For the first time in my life, I had become aware that I needed forgiveness. I needed the Saviour, Jesus, who would forgive me and deliver me from my sins. I felt so undeserving, so wretched in God's eyes!

I was amazed to see how, every day, I became more and more aware that for 24 years I had lived apart from God, living only for my pleasure and selfish interests.

The Scripture says that Jesus Christ died and was raised from the dead so that those who believe should no longer live for themselves, but for the One who died and was raised from the dead *for them*, that is, Jesus Christ (2 Corinthians 5:15).

How wonderful and vitally important this book, the Bible, is – it is God's Instruction Manual for man. The same way that a washing machine or a sewing machine, or any other machine, needs an instruction manual to show how to use it, man needs the Bible. In this wonderful book, we have the whole of God's plan for our life. Man needs a purpose and a reason for the life he lives. The proud look arrogantly to others and to this life, and cannot see the One who is above – God!

One characteristic of all the people on earth is the fact that each one of us desires to be happy and looks for happiness. What separates us from one another is the fact that some look for happiness where this cannot be found! God has created us to be happy; it's just that man, through his disobedience, has become separated from God and has become unhappy. The definition, or the recipe, for happiness is given in the Bible, Psalm 73:28: '*But as for me, it is good* [my happiness is' – Romanian translation] *to be near God!*' It is of great importance that people read and obey the Bible.

My cellmate didn't seem interested in this book, and he spent many hours watching TV. When I was arrested I had 300 Deutsche Marks with me, and this money was deposited in a personal account for me. I had filed a request to the chief guard for a TV that cost 100 DM because, in our prison section, no cell had a TV – and so this was the reason I'd decided to buy the television.

But now I no longer enjoyed the movies that the German channels were showing at night, and I realised that something unusual was happening to me. Until Uncle Gigi came to the prison and taught me from the New Testament, I had also enjoyed those kinds of movies but, after I'd heard all that I had from the Bible (words that Uncle Gigi shared with me), at night, when my cellmate was watching those movies, I would turn in my bed to face the wall and put a pillow over my head. I knew from the Scriptures that it was not good to do such things and, somehow, I felt that God did not like what my cellmate was doing.

A holy fear was growing in my heart. I wanted to get rid of that TV set, but I did not know how to do it. I would not have liked to force my cellmate, Gigi, not to watch TV anymore. I respected him, because he was a special young man, and he'd helped me on several occasions. Suddenly, a thought came to my mind: I started praying to God to help me get rid of the TV set, and, shortly after that, the brand-new TV set I had purchased stopped working!

Gigi sent it to be fixed at his expense and, even though this should not have taken too long, two months passed and the TV had not returned from the repair shop. I was jubilant, and I was amazed, at the way God had started answering my prayers. I was not sorry that the TV set was not repaired faster, but my cellmate was desperate; he could not understand what was going on, and why we had to wait so long!

Eventually Gigi asked to know what was going with the TV set. When he told the person in charge that the TV had been sent to the repairs two months before, this person was really shocked, and finally he brought us another TV set, identical to first one. My cellmate was now in a good mood again – while I was upset with what I had to put up with!

Nevertheless, not long after that, God did another miracle. One of the chief guards asked me if I wanted to go out and work. In the prison section where I was kept, there were approximately 100 prisoners. Four of them were managing this section; three received a salary and one was a volunteer. When one of them was released from prison, or was sent to another penitentiary, the fourth filled that position and another volunteer was brought in. Because one of these three prisoners had been released, a fourth volunteer was now needed. The chief guard came to me and asked me if I wanted to be a volunteer with the prisoners who were managing the section I was in. This offer took me by surprise, because I could not speak German, and I had not filed an application for this job.

The prisoners who were managing the section had special privileges compared to the others; their cell was open until 9pm, as well as other benefits. Almost everyone who was locked in had filed an application for this job but, because I could not speak German, I knew I would never get this kind of job, so I never requested it.

I was amazed, so I wanted to be sure that I understood what the guard was telling me. I tried to 'communicate' with my hands, telling him that I did not have a written application for this job; he told me, also with his hands, that it was not a problem. A few hours after we were taken to our cells, the chief guard came to my cell with

an application form, and asked me to sign it. After I
signed it, I was taken out of my cell, in which I had
spent six months together with Gigi. When I left the
cell, I gladly gave Gigi the TV set, because it was the
football (soccer) world championship, and he wanted to
watch it so much, while the only thing that interested
me was my new relationship with God. I was moved to
a new cell by myself on the ground floor of that section,
where the conditions were better compared to those for
the other prisoners.

The four inmates that were managing the section
had a head inmate who was over the other three, and
this man coordinated everything that happened and
received more money than the other two. His name
was Antonio and he was an Italian. During the six
months that I spent there, I learnt Italian quite well, as I
befriended a few Italians who were in my section.

Antonio was astonished to see me as a volunteer,
because he knew I could not speak German, and in
order to get that job you had to speak the language.
When he asked me how I'd ended up as a volunteer,
I pointed my finger to heaven and I answered him in
his language: *Dio* (God), He did this for me, for I had
become one of His children. He was amazed when he
heard my answer, and he shrugged his shoulders.

The next day I started my job. I had to sweep the floor,
wash the hallways and, after I had distributed the food,
I had to take the dishes to the kitchen. It was not very
easy for me, but I was happy I did not have to spend 23
out of 24 hours in my cell. Sometimes, though, when I
had the bucket and the rag in my hands, washing the
hallways, the devil would tempt me and whisper in my

ear: 'What has become of you, Vasile Tofan? A former champion in your country, you are now washing the hallways of this prison!' When these kinds of thoughts came into my mind, I received them with tears in my eyes...but the next moment, I would hear another voice in my heart that said: 'He who humbles himself will be lifted up, but he who lifts himself up will be humbled!' I knew these words came from God because I had read them in the Bible.

The days were passing by, like they had passed by before, but now I was freer, I had different conditions and privileges, and my cell door was open from 6am until 9pm. I could pray without being bothered, and I could read my Bible in peace. I learnt to enjoy every day I spent in that place. However, I would think often of the one I loved so dearly, with a different attitude now than the one I'd had when I was with her. I also enjoyed my daily fellowship with Uncle Gigi Sabău. I was overwhelmed by God's love, and I knew that my privileged situation was due to God.

Chapter 8

Sunday was a special day. There was a rule that we could go to visit one another, but no more than four inmates in a cell and for no longer than three and a half hours. You could visit anyone in your section, but only under the rules mentioned above. In my cell the guest of honour was Uncle Gigi Sabău; alongside him I would invite other Romanians who also enjoyed hearing the Word of God.

I was so amazed listening to Uncle Gigi share from the Scriptures, and I was also so happy to hear about God's plan for us as people, a plan made in Jesus Christ, His Son, whom He sent to our world to die in our place! Jesus Christ, the Perfect One, the Sinless One, who left the glory He had had with His Father in heaven, came to us on earth, took on Himself the burden of the sins of the world, was crucified, died, and on the third day rose from the dead. Yes, the Son of God, the Saviour of the world, was our substitute in the punishment that we deserved! How wonderful that in the good news of the gospel, we can know the whole plan of salvation!

All those who believe in the sacrifice of Jesus Christ are forgiven of all their sinful past, their soul is saved, and they become children of God and receive *eternal life* as a gift. God's great plan of salvation is presented in the Holy Scriptures, the Word of God, given – through the

Holy Spirit – to human writers, who have written the
Bible, inspired by Him, a divine and infallible Word,
having proceeded from the mouth of the Eternal God.

The three and a half hours passed like three and a
half minutes. When the guards would come and put
the key in the door, saying, '*Zeit ist abgelaufen,*' – 'Time
is up!' – I was very sad; I could not believe that the time
I had spent listening to the Word of God had passed so
quickly!

Later, I discovered in the Bible that, whenever and
wherever two or three people are gathered in His
Name, He is there with them, in their midst. When
Jesus Christ is present in a place, fellowship becomes
very special, wonderful, and time stops, or flies, and
when you realise how much time has passed, it is hard
to believe that this flew away. I could not stop thinking
of those who had been in the presence of our Saviour
when He was on earth, and I spent a few Sundays with
this sense of wonder.

I remember that, one Sunday, Uncle Gigi asked us if
we wanted to pray. His question took us by surprise
because we did not see it coming! When we heard this,
we were a little confused, because we did not know how
to pray; some of us did not even know the Lord's Prayer.
Uncle Gigi looked at us and said it was no problem, and
he asked if we would agree for him to pray for us. We
accepted, of course, and he made us kneel and close
our eyes to be able to concentrate better on our prayers.
We knelt and closed our eyes, and the next moment I
heard such a prayer that made me open my eyes to see
from where Mr Sabău was reading such a prayer! What
amazed me was the fact that Uncle Gigi had his eyes

closed and had no prayer book in his hands. I waited for him to finish, and we all said 'Amen!' and stood up.

I was the first to ask Uncle Gigi to write down for me, on a piece of paper, the prayer that he had just prayed because I liked it so much, and I wanted to learn it by heart. Uncle Gigi looked at me and told me that he hadn't learnt the prayer – it was from the heart.

He then told us a story of what had happened fifteen years before, when he was a man in bondage to alcohol, and how all the money he made was spent in a pub. He'd reached the point where his wife would collect him from the gutters in Târgoviște, his town. She was at a loss to know what else she could do for him.

Then, one day, a friend of his asked him to go with him to a house of prayer, where several believers had gathered to sing, pray and praise the Name of God. Uncle Gigi agreed and went along. When he arrived there that evening, something extraordinary happened. An indescribable joy filled his whole being as he heard a man speaking from the Word of God that Jesus, the Son of God, had come to earth to deliver people from the bondage of sin and the devil, so that from that point on, people could receive eternal life as a gift. That evening, he felt something inside that he had not felt before; when the service was over he went home with a joy that he had never experienced in his life. From that night on, he had never felt the need to drink alcohol, and he made the decision to live for God every day that he had left on this earth.

In the story that Uncle Gigi told us, he used a word that I deeply disliked: he said he made the decision to *repent*, according to God's command for all people, as it is written in the Scriptures, in Acts 17:30-31: *'In the past God overlooked such ignorance, but now he commands all people everywhere to repent. For he has set a day when he will judge the world with justice by the man he has appointed. He has given proof of this to everyone by raising him from the dead.'.*

Because it seemed to me humiliating and downright offensive to tell someone to repent, a true war started in my heart.

I knew, from Ceausescu's time, that those called *pocăiți* [a word which has a negative connotation in Romanian, meaning people who repent] were considered sect members, who were performing great atrocities. They killed children and took their blood; they went to rooms where they turned off the lights and had incredible orgies, and all sorts of similar things. This is what we were told at school and at home about people who repented. So I told Mr Sabau all this, but he started laughing and told me that these were gross lies.

Because, throughout the centuries, people who believed in God were different in their behaviour than other people, lies and all sorts of bad things were hurled at the believers. We have numerous examples in the Word of God, and he told me about John the Baptist, about Steven, about the Apostle Paul and about many others. In exactly the same way, Ceausescu's secret police and Communist government tried to blame those who gave up their sinful life and started a new life according to the Word of God.

I realised, though, that no matter how much Uncle Gigi was trying to explain what repentance was and what it meant to be a believer, I still felt embarrassed when hearing this word. More than that, I saw that some of the Romanians who were there avoided speaking to Mr Sabau, who was different to the rest of us, and they were speaking evil about him for no reason. They did not dare to laugh at me or speak evil of me, though, because they were afraid they would be introduced to my fists!

There was not a single day when I did not think about all that Uncle Gigi told me and taught me from the Bible! Reading the Scriptures carefully, I understood that I was a sinful man, and the wages for my sins was death; not a physical death, but an eternal separation from the God I felt I had started to love. The Bible gives an answer to the great existential questions that man needs to ask as long as he lives on earth: **Who are we? Where do we come from? Where are we going?**

Until I got to jail I thought I was a strong man, able to lead my life on my own, but when I read 2 Corinthians 5:15, I understood that man should no longer live for himself and for his selfish desires, but only for God. When a man lives for God, having Him as the supreme priority and placing Him first in his life, life then gains meaning, colour, charm and beauty. I'd had no idea, and it had never crossed my mind, that the fact I was healthy and strong was only because of God! I had failed to thank God for food, clothing, sight and hearing, for everything I was and had. I had thought I deserved all these things!

My desire to pray to God grew more and more in my heart, but I did not know how to do it. I woke up very early one morning, knelt down, and closed my eyes. I wanted to say something, but my mouth was clenched,

I could not articulate a word and my mind went blank. I spent a few minutes like this, hoping that I could open my mouth, but I wasn't able to articulate a single word! I stood up and I was quite sad that I wasn't able to address a prayer to God. My desire to pray came back the following days, but still with no result.

One morning I woke up, and like every other morning, I knelt down and I took a Bible in my hand, holding it close to my chest. I was kneeling and thinking about what I could possibly tell God. I do not know exactly how long passed but, suddenly, I had a thought that was like a very loud voice. This voice told me to open the Book I had in my hands.

I opened the Bible randomly, not knowing where it would open. When I looked at the right page I saw a very small title: Psalm 119. The voice that had told me to open the Book was now telling me to read. I started reading every verse from Psalm 119 and, the more I read, the more I realised that those words were just right for me, and so I turned them into a prayer. I was praying to God with the words of Psalm 119!

After I finished reading all the 176 verses of Psalm 119, I closed the book, put it on the bed, and continued to pray with my own words. Until then, I had been begging God to make a way for me to be released from jail, but now I was **asking** God not to get me out of that place sooner! I was afraid that, if I went home too soon, I would forget about Him! I was afraid that I would go back to my old habits and sinful life.

That morning, I asked God to do something with my life, to change me and make me a new person. I no longer wanted to live the way I'd lived before I got into the penitentiary. I had a burning desire to be a man pleasing to God and who would live his life the way Jesus showed us when He lived on earth.

I do not know how long I prayed, or what else I said with my words, but I know that when I finished and stood up, I felt exceedingly happy! It felt like a new heart was beating in my chest, a heart that was full of a joy and happiness I had never known before. I felt like screaming out loud for happiness! In those moments I sensed I was being delivered from selfishness, I did not hate anyone, and all the grudges I'd held against anyone were gone in an instant. It felt as if I were able to love even my worst enemy! Tears were flooding down my face and I was so happy! The embarrassment that the other inmates would call me *pocăit* was gone. I did not even care that I was imprisoned! Actually, it was not that I did not care – I cared, of course – but I felt that the tremendous inner struggle, the restlessness of my soul, which had been so overwhelming in the days and nights of my imprisonment, had mysteriously disappeared. My heart was full of a peace that I had not known before! That morning God, in His kindness, came to me and lifted the burden of my sins that I had committed throughout the years until that time. God flooded my being with peace, love and the joy of His Holy Spirit: all that Jesus Christ promised to all those who would trust Him, obey Him and follow His teachings left for us in the Holy Scriptures. I could say, without doubt, that I was the happiest man on earth! I was a born-again person!

Man has to be born again in order to enter God's Kingdom and see it. The fact that I was a born-again man was clear in my thoughts, my speech, and my desires. Before that, I had so many sinful thoughts going through my mind. I cussed and used swear words, especially when I was furious. My desires were mainly sinful and selfish.

After that morning, when I prayed to God, I saw, with great amazement, that there were no dirty words coming out of my mouth! My thoughts were now mainly directed to God and His Word and, in all my desires, I wanted to be pleasing to God and live the way He wanted me to live. The words in 2 Corinthians 5:17 became true for me: *'Therefore, if anyone is in Christ, the new creation has come: The old has gone, the new is here!'*

Until I read and believed the Holy Scriptures I had been blind, but God healed my sight and the eyes of my soul started to see what they could not see until then. Here is what the Apostle Paul says to the Ephesians in his epistle:

As for you, you were dead in your transgressions and sins, in which you used to live when you followed the ways of this world and of the ruler of the kingdom of the air, the spirit who is now at work in those who are disobedient. All of us also lived among them at one time, gratifying the cravings of our flesh and following its desires and thoughts. Like the rest, we were by nature deserving of wrath. But because of his great love for us, God, who is rich in mercy, made us alive with Christ even when we were dead in transgressions—it is by grace you have been saved. -Ephesians 2:1-5

God had performed a miracle in me!

Chapter 9

When I saw Uncle Gigi I told him what had happened to me, and he said: 'Greater things you will see and greater joys you will experience!' The days that followed were days in which God overwhelmed me with His love and kindness. That morning, in the spring of 1994, I was born again; I was born of God. How do I know this? The way I lived every day was proof. I could not talk dirty anymore, and I could not even listen to the swearing or the vulgar words the others were using. I found no pleasure in listening to the adventures and filthy things the other Romanians were bragging about in which they found great pleasure. I received a new power, like I had not known before, to be able to talk with the other Romanians about what was written in the gospel. It was so clear to me that another Vasile Tofan had been born in that penitentiary! I began to understand the words of Jesus to Nicodemus, in the Gospel of John, chapter 3: *'No one can enter the Kingdom of God unless they are born again.'*

As time passed by, I was falling in love more and more with the Word of God, and I was so happy when I was able to spend time talking with God in prayer. When I prayed to God, telling Him everything that was on my heart, He would fill my soul with His peace and solid trust that He was in control of my life. The Word

of God, the Bible, became the mirror in which I had
to look every day. When I read the New Testament,
especially the four Gospels, I discovered I was poor,
blind and naked, and that a huge wall, built with my
sins, was standing between me and God. I understood
why I could not see myself as I was until I got to this
place, because I had been comparing myself with other
people around me.

When you want to see who you are, and you
compare yourself with others, you will always have
the tendency to believe that you are the best and the
greatest. The New Testament, though, paints the image
of the Man Jesus Christ. Anyone who wants to see his
true condition needs to compare himself with the One
who came down from heaven and made Himself a man
for us; He took on Himself all the sins of the world,
and made peace between rebellious man and God the
Father. Only when he stands in the light of the Word of
God can a man can see his true image and identity.

In Romans chapter 3, the Apostle Paul, guided by
the Holy Spirit, describes the lowly condition of all of
mankind. What a pity that most people do not read, or
do not make time to read, the Holy Scriptures! Because
of that, most people live far away from God, and do not
know Him. And, because most people do not read the
Bible, they have created false images and ideas about
God.

Until I was imprisoned, I also thought it was normal
to lie, to talk dirty, to cheat on your wife and many
other things...I did not consider it was so bad to lie,
especially if the lie was to your profit. I had not known,
for so many years, that God did not create the mouth to

speak dirty, to lie or to drink alcohol and then commit felonies. God did not create the eyes for pornography, violent movies, or any other filthy activities. God has created all things to bring Him glory, magnificence, honour, and admiration. Man must praise and thank his Creator and, when man does that, he becomes the happiest man on earth. A locomotive cannot run outside the tracks; and a ship is of no use unless it floats on the seas and oceans; and a fish can only live in water. In the same way, a man is the happiest when he lives totally for God.

The days I spent in prison were days when the sun was shining so brightly for me! I was aware that each new day was a gift from God for me, and I was doing everything joyfully as unto God. It was no longer hard for me to wash the hallways, to sweep the floors, to take the dishes to the kitchen, because I was thinking what price the Lord Jesus had paid for me so that I could be saved from my sins and have eternal life. I did not have enough words to thank God for all this!

Antonio, the Italian who was my boss, started noticing the joy I had almost every day in my heart. I started a new habit; after lunch was served, and after I took the dishes to the kitchen, I would go to my cell and pray to God – and I did this every day.

Antonio noticed that, after every lunch, I would disappear to my cell. One day, he wanted to know what I was doing in my cell, and he came and tried to get into the cell. But, because I was kneeling in prayer, with my feet against the door, he could not get in. He did not give up so easily, and pushed the door once again, and so I had to stand up and open the door.

After he entered, he looked at me with amazement, and asked me in Italian: 'What are you doing here?' I answered him, a little bit irritated, that I was talking with God. His amazement grew more, and he asked: 'How come you are talking with God, are you crazy?' I realised he could not understand what I was saying, so I told him I was praying. He suddenly became very interested and asked me to share more about God, and so I talked with him, and I told him everything God was giving me and was placing in my heart to tell him. After we finished talking, Antonio seemed very pleased with our conversation, and I was so glad, giving thanks to God for all he was doing for me in that place.

The guards also noticed my behaviour, and were thrilled with everything they saw me doing. The joy I had in my heart was reflected on my face, and this could not go unnoticed. Uncle Gigi was also very happy with all he could see happening and, anytime we had a chance, we thanked God together. The time went by very quickly and, after seven months, I received my sentence for the robbery in Wolfsburg, from the court in Braunschweig: the sentence was two years! Strangely enough, I was not desperate, knowing that God would help to get me back home when He thought I was ready to leave that place. My mood and attitude changed; I was imprisoned and yet I was free, convinced that I was in God's school and that I would stay there until I had learned all the lessons that needed to be learnt.

For my first robbery a new trial in another city was needed.

In the evenings I would meet with Uncle Gigi at the rec room in our section, and we would share positive thoughts that were interesting to both of us. When I did not understand something from the Bible, Uncle Gigi would explain it to me straightaway. The other inmates were smoking and watching TV, but my fellow believer and I talked about things that were written in the Holy Scriptures. When we went to bed at night, we were so happy and had amazing joy in our hearts, while the other inmates tried to find their joy in bad jokes that targeted someone in the group, or something similar.

At 9pm all the cells were locked. When I went back to my cell, and the guard that locked my cell had wished me good night, I would kneel and give thanks to God for the whole day and for all the help I had received from Him. I could feel God's presence everywhere, and I was confident that He was with me, blessing me in all that I was doing in that tough place. I had read in the Gospel of Matthew the words of Jesus, and I was praying to fulfil them in that place: *'Do to others what you would have them do to you'* (Matthew 7:12). The guards were very pleased with my behaviour there. They saw that I acted differently to the other prisoners...but they did not understand this was because of God! If I had not been born again, and if God had not revealed Himself to me in His Word, my behaviour would have been like the others' – whether Romanians or other nationalities. I gave thanks to God for everything He was doing for me.

It was absolutely wonderful to see that Antonio was changing little by little! Until I shared with him from the Word of God, he was a guy whom everybody hated; he acted despicably, he would make us give him what we had if it was something that he liked, and he was rude and difficult to put up with. But, after I shared the Gospel with him and started praying with him, his behaviour changed, and the inmates were amazed when they saw Antonio speaking nicely and sharing the food equally. When I spent time alone with God, I thanked Him for everything He was doing in that place. God was working with signs and wonders.

One day, I shared with Gigi Sabău, who had become my older brother in the faith, that I had a terrible pain in both of my elbows. With the slightest effort, an intense pain would start in my arms, so that I could not move them along my body. If I wanted to lift something up, I could not do it until the pain was gone, and it was a pain that lasted for about an hour.

Uncle Gigi said that we should pray to God with the faith that He could heal me. One night, after the guards locked us in at 9pm, I knelt and prayed that I would be healed, and Uncle Gigi was also praying in his cell for my healing. I do not remember how long I prayed that night, but the next day I got up and wanted to check if God had heard me. So I did ten push-ups. Usually, until that morning, if I did such a thing, the pain would start instantaneously. I stood up and I realised I had no pain in my elbows! I continued lifting the iron table in my cell a few times. No pain whatsoever! I went to the gym and did some exercises with the 70kg weight – and the pain was no longer there. I leaped for joy, shouting to Uncle Gigi: 'God has healed me, God has healed me!' I was both amazed and happy! God overwhelmed me every day in all He did, and through the help He gave me, both in earthly things and spiritual things.

Chapter 10

Eight months had passed since I was imprisoned. One day, Uncle Gigi received a letter from the German DA. Because I did not know German very well I gave it to someone who could read and translate the letter. I found out that Uncle Gigi was going to be released from prison and receive a sum of money, because the German police had no case or evidence against him. We were both amazed at this letter. It was true what Uncle Gigi had said in the beginning, that he was not guilty of anything that could make him a prisoner – and this letter confirmed all he had said. It was difficult for me to say good-bye to this man God had sent to this place to open my eyes, so that I was able to turn from darkness to light. I was glad and sad at the same time; glad that Uncle Gigi was going to be set free and he would go back to Romania to his wife and children, but sad that I was left alone, with no fellow believer.

During the following days Uncle Gigi was set free, but before he left, he shook my hand and told me not to be afraid and to trust God. He knew that there were going to be trials of my new-found faith; but he advised me to fight with the weapons the Scriptures gave, among which fasting and prayer were the first.

After Uncle Gigi left, I tried to find someone among the Romanian prisoners who would keep me company,

and also to share with him what was written in the
Bible. I was amazed to see that all those who knew
Uncle Gigi did not want to hear anything about God.
Not even Gigi Cherar, from Gura Humorului, who
had seemed so interested at first! The Romanians with
whom I talked told me they wanted to come back to
Germany for more burglaries and to continue stealing.
I was even more amazed to hear from them that their
god was money!

Every time I heard the plans they had for the future
my heart was very sad. Not one of the Romanians in
prison wanted to hear about the words of the New
Testament! What was even more amazing was that all
believed they were Christians, but had no clue what
that meant. I remembered the words that Uncle Gigi
had left with me before he left: 'Fasting and prayer are
two of the most powerful weapons that are available
for every Christian who wants to be victorious in the
life of faith!'

Starting from the next day, I decided not to eat or
drink during the day or during the night, because I
had a burning desire that God would change the hearts
of the Romanians who rejected the Good News of the
gospel. The first day I did not eat or drink anything; the
next day I did the same, and the third day the same as
well. I had not fasted to this extent until then! God was
the One who strengthened me to fast.

During the evening of the third day, something
unusual happened; I felt God's presence in my cell. My
heart was filled with an indescribable joy, and I could
hear the following words in my inner being, saying:
'Don't be afraid, I am with you!' These were words that

God poured into my heart. After these three days I went to the Romanians that were there, and I found I could speak to them about the love of God shown in His Son, Jesus Christ. I was so glad that I could share for more than two hours without interruptions or opposition! In the evening, when I went to pray, I thanked God for the power He had given me in sharing the Gospel.

In the following days, God opened the heart of a Romanian who had been transferred from another penitentiary. This man was from Bucharest, and you will not believe this, but his name was Gigi. After a heated discussion with him, I recommended he read the New Testament. Gigi from Bucharest had a false, totally wrong image about God, because – like I did in the beginning – he had started reading the Bible in the Old Testament. Everything he read there created a strong repulsion in his heart towards God, and I was glad when he decided to read the New Testament. I prayed for him every day, and my great joy was the fact that we had started talking, and Gigi had questions that I could answer with God's help.

My prayers regarding Gigi received an answer. We started to pray and study the Scriptures together, and Gigi's heart opened more and more to God.

After we had spent three months together, Gigi from Bucharest became a new man! Through the help of the Holy Spirit, the Word of God made him see his sins, which he regretted, and he wanted to be forgiven. Before he was transferred to a new penitentiary, Gigi received the joy of salvation and believed with all his heart in Jesus Christ, who gave His life for his sins, too.

After we'd hugged and prayed together, I entrusted

him to the hand of God, asking him not to forget all that God had done for him in that tough place where we'd met. I was happy that Gigi from Bucharest had found peace and happiness in God; but I was also sad because he left and I was alone again, with no fellow believer. I could not rejoice with Antonio in the same way I was able to rejoice with Uncle Gigi or with Gigi from Bucharest. I was praying for Antonio, and I wanted him to grow in the faith, too.

One day, Antonio came to me and said: 'I know you talk with God. Would you like to ask Him what will happen tomorrow at my trial?' I smiled, patted him on his shoulder, and I said I would do that. Antonio had been imprisoned for rape; in Germany rape was severely punished, because prostitution was legal. He had little chance of being set free.

That night, when the guards locked our cells, I kneeled to thank God and pray, but I had no peace in my heart; I felt something was wrong, and I had done something that was not pleasing to God. I stopped and asked God to search my heart to discover my sin and what was disrupting my peace with my Creator. Suddenly, I remembered the careless pat on Antonio's shoulder, assuring him that I would ask God about the outcome of his trial the next day. I'd behaved as if God was at my disposal, ready to do everything I commanded Him to do! I repented, and I asked for forgiveness for the light way in which I had approached God.

I started praying to God with tears in my eyes, asking Him to release me from the predicament I was in. What was I going to say to Antonio the next morning? I prayed fervently and for a long time, and yet I received no answer from God. There was a lot of restlessness in my heart, but eventually I fell asleep, as I was very tired. The next morning I woke up at 5am and I was smiling because I had the answer for Antonio in my heart. I jumped out of bed directly onto my knees, thanking God with all my heart for His kindness and mercy that He was pouring on me.

At 6am, when the guard opened our cells, Antonio was right there in front of my cell. With no introduction, he asked me directly: 'What did *Dio* tell you?' I looked at him and I said: 'Antonio, here is what God has told me to say to you: "If you truly believe in your heart that God is helping you today to be free, you will be free!"' I emphasised that God does not look at what we say but at the heart.

He looked at me intently and signaled to me to follow him into his cell. When we entered there we both knelt and prayed to God, each of us in his own language. I gave thanks to God, once again, for the answer that He had given me in my heart for Antonio. After we prayed and stood up, Antonio looked at me and said: 'I believe with all my heart that today God will help me to be free.' Honestly, I did not believe what he said, but I assured him, once again, that God looks at the heart – and then we each continued with our chores.

Antonio left for the court, and I carried on with my daily chores. After I had served lunch and finished all the chores, I went back to my cell; I prayed and lay on my bed. I know I was not sleeping but was meditating on the Word of God when I felt the hand of the guard who was on duty that day on my shoulder. I opened my eyes and I saw him smiling: 'Rejoice, because you have now been promoted. You will no longer be a volunteer, you will receive money. Antonio has been released!' I jumped out of bed and I could not believe my ears. 'Antonio, free?' And so it was!

In the days that followed, God spoke to my heart and assured me that what He'd done for Antonio was a miracle. With Antonio leaving, I was being promoted and I was going to get money for my work. So, from the fourth prisoner, I was becoming the third, and my place was vacant now for another volunteer. I was happy because I was going to get 220 DM every month and, in Romania, that amount of money meant something. This money was put in an account as I did not have anywhere to spend it.

God was going to amaze me even further and show me why he had worked that way. My wife had lost her job at some point. It was around Christmas of 1994, and she was in a difficult situation. When I managed to talk with her, she said she was sad because she had no money and needed it to go shopping for the holidays. With the help of a Romanian brother who was a German citizen, and who had received the right to visit me once a week, I managed to withdraw the 500 DM I had in my account and sent it to my lovely wife, who was very glad.

I praised God for this miracle and for the wonderful way in which He had arranged everything. How wonderful it is to be a child of the Creator of the Universe! He provides for the smallest detail, and no hair falls to the ground without Him knowing it.

Immediately after I had all these blessings from God, I received notification from the German DA that I was going to be moved to another penitentiary, much bigger than this one, because now I was a convicted prisoner. The penitentiary in Braunschweig, where I had stayed for a year, was a transitory one where one could not spend more than a year, according to German law.

The brother who helped me to send the money home came from Mediaș, and his name was Tiberiu Ursu. He was a special man who visited me every Friday because he had permission to come and counsel us on spiritual issues. He was a man that God used wonderfully, and many times he would bring us cakes that his wife had made at home.

I spent New Year's Eve in Wolfenbuttel Penitentiary. I was glad that I was a born-again Christian from the beginning of 1995, a child of God, but I was so sad that I had to spend another year alone, without the one that my heart longed for. I remember that, at midnight, when people were celebrating the beginning of a new year, I was praying and pouring my whole heart out to God. There was joy in my heart, but also a lot of grief. I was thinking of the days when I was near the one that God had given me as a wife, but whom I did not know how to love or cherish. I was thinking how much it would have meant to know the Word of God when I was at home! If I had known then what God wants and asks from us, His people, I would not have suffered like I was doing here, in prison, far from my dear ones.

There is a big hole in the heart of every man, which he tries to fill throughout the years as he thinks appropriate: alcohol, fun, love affairs, riches, winning titles, status and so on. The more man pursues these things, the bigger the hole in his heart gets – wider and deeper. Why? Because this huge hole in man's heart can be filled only by God; only God can fill the emptiness with the result that man becomes whole again, knowing the true meaning of life.

When, in the Garden of Eden, Adam saw he was naked, he tried to cover his nakedness with an apron of leaves. Even though he had a cover now, he did not have the courage to stand before God, like he did before. This time, shame and fear had taken hold of him. He knew he was naked and he also knew that the apron of leaves could not cover his true nakedness, which was found in his soul due to his disobedience to the commands of the Creator.

In the same way today, there are so many people who are trying to cover their nakedness under the mask of religion. But no matter what this is, religion cannot cover or fill the hole in people's hearts, and religion cannot connect you with God. Jesus Christ, His Son, is the only One who can connect you to God. God is not a religion, He is a Person who desires so much to have communion with the people He created. In order to accomplish this, man needs to believe in Jesus Christ, the One who is the Way, the Truth and the Life.

Until I ended up in prison I had been blind, but Jesus restored my sight, helping me to understand His Word and to live it out in the power of the Holy Spirit. The Bible is the Word of God, and is the only book in the world that can be called this. The Bible is not just simply a book, it is a collection of books in which God reveals Himself to the man He created. The Bible is not a science dissertation, even though it contains proven scientific truths; there is nothing in the Bible that can be shown as false. The Bible is a divine gift made to man, a heavenly and kingly gift, in which God pulls away the curtain that hides Him from our eyes. In the Bible, God speaks to man today, if man is only willing to listen to the One who speaks from heaven.

Chapter 11

Wolfenbuttel Penitentiary had many visitors because, in its inner courts, there was a museum. It was there that Hitler ordered that many Jews be beheaded, and all the names of those who had been executed were written on the wall of a room. The guillotine was still in place, and the cells were still preserved where those condemned to death waited until the sentence was accomplished.

Wolfenbuttel Penitentiary had three buildings, which were the three sections for the prisoners. One of the sections had better conditions than the other two; its cells could be compared to the rooms of a modest hotel, and the food seemed as if it were from a fancy restaurant! The conditions here were far better than in Braunschweig. I was put into one of these cells along with a German guy.

I only stayed there for a short while. Two weeks later, I was moved to Haus (House) IV, where there were many Romanians. Haus IV was a transitory place, and it was from there that Romanians who did not stay longer than 6-8 months were expelled to Romania. Because I had a very good report from Braunschweig Penitentiary, the head of that section put me alone in a cell. This was very good for me, because I could pray whenever I wanted, and I could be alone in God's presence. All those in Haus IV knew I was a professional boxer. This section accommodated prisoners from different countries: Germans, Turks, Africans, Russians, Moldovans, Arabs, Indians and Romanians. As a result, there were many conflicts among the convicts, and, anytime a conflict arose, all prisoners were locked in until evening. This was very bad, because then we could not walk and do the activities that helped avoid the stress there.

Shortly after I got there, I received the right to work. Every morning I was taken to a room where I fixed the metal part to the files that came from a different place, and I received a lot of money for such a little job. Part of the money was put in a personal account, which gave me the opportunity to go to the shop inside the prison, and the rest of the money was kept in an account to which no-one had access. The money that gathered in that account was mine the moment I finished my time in prison and I was released from the penitentiary. The money that someone received when he finished his time in prison was meant to help him get by until he could find work. It was a very well thought-out system by the Ministry of Justice in Germany and, if one spent several years in prison, the money in his account would be of real help until he could find work.

The first Romanian I met there was a man from a town near Bacău; his name was Viorel. He told me there were many Romanians on the first floor. One day, I went to meet the Romanians on there, and I introduced myself and sat on a bed. After I had listened to the nonsense they were talking, I spoke about Jesus and what it meant to be a real Christian. It was hard not to notice the amazement on their faces, and some were even listening intently to what I was sharing. After

some time, I went back to my cell. Viorel came after me
and told me how everything he had heard had made a
great impression on him. Because he was in a cell with
no Romanians, he asked me to let him stay with me in
my cell. I did not oppose this idea, and after I spoke to
the head of our section, Viorel got his belongings and
moved in with me. I used this opportunity to share with
him all that God put on my heart and in my mouth to
tell him. I was glad to see the interest Viorel had in the
gospel and we ended up praying together, reading the
Bible together, and rejoicing in God's goodness.

Because we had so much time available, Viorel
opened his heart and told me how he had ended up
in Germany. I was impressed to hear his story. He had
been a newlywed and was married to a woman from
his home village. There was a rumour there that one
could make good money in Germany without a lot of
risk. Along with his wife he came to a city in Germany,
where he was advised to lie and say he was persecuted
by the authorities in Romania, and that that was why
he had a bad life there. If he signed such a declaration,
he would receive an amount of money from Social
Services, which was about ten times more than a
salary in Romania. After some time, he would then
go to another city, and he would register again under
a false name...and so on. This is how Viorel and his
wife managed to gather a lot of money, which they then
sent back to Romania. This scam did not last for too
long, because the German authorities discovered it and
imprisoned him.

Worse than that was the fact that his wife, a young
woman from the countryside, was free. Because of this

situation – he in prison and she at large – Viorel was tormented by the idea of how she would manage by herself, and so he was praying every day to God for his wife. One day, he received a letter from the German authorities, and because he could not read German, he asked someone to translate his letter. After he had heard what the letter said, he came back to his cell as white as a sheet. What had happened? The German police had arrested his wife too, and sent her to a women's prison. After some checks, the German authorities had discovered the true identity of Viorel's wife. My cellmate was desperate, telling me that, if his father-in-law found out where his daughter was, it would be very bad for him.

I tried to calm him down and exhorted him to trust God, and we started praying fervently for this situation. I was asking God to have mercy and show Viorel His kindness and grace, because it was a critical situation that could make anyone very sick. It did not take long! Viorel received a letter from his wife, and to my amazement, his wife was encouraging him not to worry because of her. This letter was an answer to our prayers.

One day, Viorel received another letter from the German authorities, which stated that both he and his wife were going to be expelled from Germany in February. That letter was sent in the beginning of December 1994. Viorel did not like the content of this letter; in fact he was quite desperate about this news. The people back home did not know where they were, and he had written to them and said they would be spending the winter holidays together. How would he explain them not being there for the holidays? He was terrified, thinking about what would happen to him if his father-in-law found out that his daughter had been put in prison in Germany!

I tried again to calm him, and we continued to pray and trust God. After two weeks, God answered our prayers again; the German authorities sent him a new letter stating that, together with his wife, he was going to be sent to Romania on 22 December! When he heard that, Viorel was overjoyed. He didn't know how to thank God for this answer, and I was also rejoicing with him. I praised God for His kindness, and I told Viorel not to forget the goodness that God had poured on him! Usually people forget so quickly when God does good to them, and they consequently forget to thank and praise Him.

In the Gospel of Luke, chapter 17, the Scripture tells us about ten lepers that the Lord Jesus healed. Even though all of them were healed, only one turned back to thank Him. What a pity that people do not know how to thank God for all the good they experience which comes from Him!

On 22 December 1994, Viorel left Haus IV to go back to Romania. He was very happy and I hugged him and prayed for him. Maybe one day I will meet him again; if not in this life, maybe in God's Kingdom, if both of us remain faithful to the end!

After Viorel left I did not take on anyone else in my cell. I continued to pray every day, and as days went by, He kept pouring more love and mercy on me. The following days my thoughts were with Viorel, and I remembered the miracles God did with him and for him. I remembered the fervent prayers that Viorel prayed to God for his situation; sometimes, when I woke up at night, I used to find Viorel kneeling in prayer, and he would pray for two or three hours. The Apostle Paul wrote to the Thessalonians, *'Pray continually'* (1 Thessalonians 5:17). The predicament that had confronted Viorel made him look for God's face and His help. In spite of these aspects, I was wondering in my heart if Viorel would fulfil the promises he had made to the Lord. In His kindness, God gives rain and sunshine, and He makes food grow which is necessary for both people and animals. Nevertheless, people are so mean and respond with so much wickedness and appalling deeds to God's kindness. And this happens because few people really know God. Very few people read the Holy Scriptures, and even fewer try to live by it.

God is a loving Father who desires to have fellowship with man, the crown of His creation. In the same way that a father rejoices over his child when the child respects and loves him, God rejoices over the man who obeys Him.

In the Garden of Eden, I believe the devil put the thought that God does not love him into man's heart, and I see this as one of the reasons he tempted Eve to eat from the tree of good and evil. What would have happened if man had eaten from the tree of life? Why did God later stop him eating from this tree as well? If man had eaten from the tree of life, then the tragedy would have been that, knowing good, he would not have been able to do it; and knowing evil, he would not have been able to avoid evil! Why? Because man had been created from the dust, and what is flesh remains flesh, and what is spirit remains spirit. God had to redeem man first from the curse of sin, and then man had to be born again, through the supernatural work of the Holy Spirit, and receive a new godly nature. Only this way can man do good and shun evil. What a great plan of salvation God prepared for fallen man! Only through our Saviour, Jesus Christ, can man find his way to God and into the Kingdom of Heaven.

Man has been created to live near God and for God and this brings man true happiness, joy and fulfilment. Just as a little child is dependent on his parents, in the same way man needs to be dependent on God. It is this dependence that the devil is trying to destroy, whispering in man's ear that he can do it alone and lead his life by himself. That is impossible!

Looking around us, we can see how much harm man does to himself. People know that cigarettes are bad for your health, and yet they produce them and smoke them! People know that alcohol is bad, and yet they drink heavily. People know that fornication is a sin, and yet they live in sin...and I could give many more examples.

The man that turns his back on God destroys himself. People want to live independently, but this is how a child would behave towards his parents at the age of five or six, telling them that he can live his life without them! Just as this thought of the child is childish and suicidal, it's the same way with the man who thinks he can live independently of God. The child might live, but he would encounter all sorts of obstacles, and the devil would set all sorts of traps for him, into which, sooner or later, he would fall and get hurt and suffer a great deal.

Why was I in prison when I was just 25 years of age? Why was I not able to avoid such a drama in my life? Because I thought I could manage my life alone, because I did not have the power to avoid evil, being attracted like iron filings to a magnet; and more than that – and also very serious and unobtainable – I did not have the power to do good!

Chapter 12

After Viorel left I befriended a German who was in that prison. I was glad to see that this man, who was older than me, had a great deal of biblical knowledge. I was also very glad that he could speak Italian. As I could not speak much German we communicated in Italian, which I was mastering quite well, as I mentioned before. His name was Uwe Paschen.

After some time together I found out the story of his life. When he was free he'd had a covenant with God and attended a Protestant church. He was a businessman, but because he did not obey God fully, he ended up in prison. This is what happens when we break God's rules. Because He loves us, God disciplines us, like a father with his child. When a father punishes the child, this is proof of his love for him – and the same happened to Uwe.

After he ended up in prison he analysed his life and discovered the mistakes he had made. I was very happy with the things I shared with this man and we ended up praying together, eating together, and spending a lot of time together.

Uwe worked with the team that managed Haus IV. The team leader was a Pole who was very interested in any 'business' that could be pursued in that place. Because he coordinated all that happened, he managed to get quite a handsome profit from all sorts of different activities. Those who wanted extra favours, starting with food, talked to this Pole. No wonder most inmates did not like him.

One day, Uwe suggested that I join this Pole's team. They had heard that, at Braunschweig, I had worked in the team that was in charge of the maintenance of the detention department, and that I had been a good addition there. Because this proposal would enable me to spend more time with Uwe, I accepted. I very quickly fitted in really well with all the things that required my attention. The inmates knew that I was a Christian and loved God, and most of them appreciated me and respected me. Some of them came to me for advice, or an opinion, and through this, I came to know a young Romanian who was in prison for robbery. When he came to Germany he had stayed in the house of a Romanian who was a German citizen. This man had offered him a lot of support, helping him in various ways. Mastered by his passion to get rich as quickly as possible, no matter what the means, this young man robbed the man who had opened his house to him. He stole a gold necklace and 7,000 DM and, on his way out, he tied up the owner with wire. If it had not been for a neighbour who came to his house, this could have ended very badly. This man filed a complaint to the police department and, after a while, the young man was caught, arrested and put in prison. Soon a trial was going to take place.

This young man, hearing that I was a religious man and devoted to God, wanted to find out from me how he should behave and what he should say at his trial.

I listened to him very carefully and I prayed for him. Because he was insistent on a piece of advice, after I prayed, I told him to admit his guilt and not to hide the truth. I advised him to tell the authorities that he regretted his actions, and that this had happened in a moment of insanity, and that he was sorry for everything that had happened.

I noticed that he read the scriptures and that he had the desire to repent of all his bad deeds. I met several times with this soul who wanted to know God.

Before he left for his trial he came and told me that the other Romanians had advised him not to admit the truth and not to heed my advice, because it was bad advice and totally unrealistic. I told him I could not decide for him, but he alone was the one to make the right decision.

I was careful to tell him that the scriptures say that Jesus, the Saviour, is Light and Truth. After I told him all this he left for the court. He was determined to lie and made the mistake of taking the Bible with him, not knowing that it says: '*Do not be deceived: God cannot be mocked. A man reaps what he sows*' (Galatians 6:7). He made sure everybody saw the Bible, including the judges. What perversity there is in man's heart who thinks that, in the same way he fools people, he can fool God!

In the evening, he came back from the trial with his soul torn to pieces due to his sentence – seven years in prison! He cried and wailed like a baby because he had listened to the advice of the other Romanians and not mine, which was to admit the truth.

No one can fool God; a man reaps what he sows! You

walk in the light, you become light; you walk in the darkness, you become darkness. God is on the side of those who live in truth, and all those who have lived in truth, and nothing but the truth, even to the cost of their lives, have been blessed by God.

Not long after that this young man was moved to a different penitentiary, because his sentence was no longer appropriate for this penitentiary; in Haus IV were only prisoners who had a maximum of two-year sentences. I felt sorry for that young man, but I had had a chance to tell him to turn to God and repent of his sins.

After this story I meditated on the words of the scriptures regarding the two thieves on the cross; one of them admitted his guilt before God, while the other one refused to admit his condition and the darkness in which he found himself. As a result of his repentance, one of the thieves crucified together with Jesus Christ reached heaven, while the other one, whose heart was hardened, missed the last chance that he had to save his soul. People are like that; some repent, admitting their condition and sins before God, and others are stubborn in their madness, thinking they are someone important.

In the Acts of the Apostles there is a story about an Ethiopian eunuch who left everything and started to search after God. Even though he was a high official, an important man in the Ethiopian queen's kingdom, he humbled himself to the point that he welcomed Philip into his chariot, a simple and insignificant man, to explain to him the passage of scripture he was reading. It did not matter to him that he was 'someone' and the one who came with him in his chariot was a 'nobody' from almost all human points of view. Because he humbled himself and admitted that he was nothing without God, God saved his soul, and the eunuch went back home full of joy. Jesus Christ came down from heaven and humbled Himself, becoming like a man: *'Who, being in very nature God, did not consider equality with God something to be used to his own advantage.'* He obeyed God to the point of death, even death on a cross. Therefore God exalted Him to the highest place, and today He is at the right hand of the Father interceding for us (Philippians 2:6-10).

There was a rumour in the hallways of Haus IV that the Pole in charge of maintenance was going to be released. Everyone wondered who would be the person to take his place and be the *hausarbeiter* (this was the name of his job), and all the prisoners wanted this position. The salary was 320 DM a month, you had a special cell, and all the goodies were at your disposal. The food there was very good, but unfortunately, you never received as much as you would have liked. The surplus food became 'exchange currency', and those who wanted an extra portion had to 'pay', whether it be in cigarettes, perfume, clothes or money. The one who was *hausarbeiter* had huge privileges, among which was the privilege to be able to talk to the guards on that section, who favoured and respected him.

One day, the chief of Haus IV came to my cell and suggested I should take this position that was about to become vacant. I said no from the beginning, telling him that I did not want to have problems with the other inmates because of the conflicts that might arise. There were times when there was not enough food in the kitchen, and you had to share it so that everyone would receive some and be content with that. There were often disputes among the prisoners, and in addition to that, the person in charge was held accountable if dishes were missing, or sports equipment, or other things that were available there. One time, a certain *hausarbeiter* received an extra six months' detention added to his initial sentence because something had been stolen and he was accused of negligence. Knowing all this, I did not want to have extra headaches with such additional responsibilities; and I truly wanted to live peacefully and in harmony with all the prisoners in Haus IV until I was released.

After some time, the head guard came to my cell again with the same proposal; again I said no. There was such a struggle in me, and I wanted to know where this tempting offer came from – God or the evil one. I started praying, asking God what to do. I asked Him to help me understand His will, speaking clearly and on my level of understanding. The third time, when the head guard came to me, he was very upset and he told me: 'If you do not agree to become *hausarbeiter*, I will move you to a penitentiary where there are no Romanians!' The words of the guard helped me understand that the offer came from God. How did I know? Because Haus IV was a transitory penitentiary, where many Romanians were brought in, and it was a special opportunity to share the gospel with as many Romanians as possible – and Romanian was the best language for me to share the gospel. If I was moved to a penitentiary with no Romanians, then sharing the gospel would have become a lot harder. More than that, when I accepted, I felt a deep peace in my heart and I was fully convinced that it was God's will for me to accept this position. When you do something against God's will, the heart is troubled and loses peace and joy.

Right after my appointment as the *hausarbeiter*, I had permission to bring together the work team just as I pleased. Because I was Romanian, I took Romanians and Moldovans (who spoke Romanian). Even though I was their boss, and had only to coordinate their work, I wanted to be an example to the others, so I worked alongside them, with no exception. When food was served, it was shared equally among the prisoners, and the surplus was shared out in the same way; I started with those on the ground floor, then I continued with the first floor, until everyone had received an equal share. This approach could not be overlooked, either by the prisoners or the guards who assisted us, when we shared out the food. Everybody noticed that I did not do 'business' with the surplus, and this made the prisoners respect me even more.

All the people in Haus IV knew I was a Christian and a child of God, and, because of my faith, I behaved this way. All this made me give more thanks and praise to God. I knew I was blessed, and in that place I received the wisdom I needed from God as I prayed every day for what I had to do during that day. God had made me like Joseph, from the Old Testament, when he was in prison. The guards would come and talk to me, and their respect for me was visible. All the activity in Haus IV was led by the grace and power of God. Misunderstandings among the prisoners were not so heated anymore, and fights were very rare. With

God's help, I managed to create a pleasant and friendly environment in Haus 4. I was rejoicing in God's love, I was rejoicing in the respect of the prisoners, and I was also rejoicing at the respect of those in leadership. Our section was spotless, extremely clean, which had not happened before! This is what the leadership of Haus 4 confessed and admitted.

On Saturdays and Sundays I had long conversations with the Romanians from the Word of God, and I was happy to see how God gave me grace and wisdom to be able to answer all their questions.

In prison, I met children from Christian families who had never turned to the true faith, and they were amazed, and happy, to listen to me there, speaking from the Word of God. The guards noticed that the Romanians were no longer starting scandals, and that the misunderstandings among the Romanians were fewer and fewer. They were all impressed with what God was giving me in my heart to speak to them from the Holy Scriptures, and I was so happy with all that God was doing in His grace and mercy in Haus IV. The word written in Proverbs 16:7 was fulfilled in that place. *'When the Lord takes pleasure in anyone's way, he causes their enemies to make peace with them.'* I lived out the truth of this verse there, where God was so present and showed He was with me in such a palpable way. I didn't have enough words to thank God for all He was doing there.

Because I had become a child of God and an enemy of the evil one, I also had trials; these have the purpose of strengthening us in faith, and of making us more determined to get closer to God. The same way that gold is refined through fire, so man's faith needs the fire of trials, because this is how it becomes a living and strong faith.

Chapter 13

One day a Yugoslavian prisoner, a drug addict, was brought in. From the first day I met him, this man hated me. In fact he could not stand anyone, and argued with everybody, because he was no longer taking drugs and his mental condition was deplorable.

One morning, at breakfast, he wanted white bread. In this section, the white bread was portioned and distributed only to people who had the doctor's permission. If a prisoner could not eat black bread, he was given white bread. In this case, with the Yugoslavian, it was just a fad. Black bread was far better than white bread, but some did not want black bread under any circumstances. Of course, I received more portions of white bread from the kitchen, but I did not want to grant the Yugoslavian's wish, because of his unreasonable behaviour.

However, God wanted to teach me a lesson on what it meant to love my enemy. It is so easy to love the one who loves you, and to do good to those who do good to you! But it is so hard to love the one who does not love you, and to do good to those who harm you!

Because the Yugoslavian showed hatred and contempt towards me right from the first day he got there, my heart was closed to him and I could not like him at all. There came difficult days with this new prisoner;

he would give me a hard time, mock me and say dirty words to me. Sometimes I was tempted to take revenge, but every time the Spirit of God would stop me.

One day, there was a conflict between a female guard and a black prisoner. Because the tension was extreme, I prayed and intervened, taking the black prisoner into one of the cells, explaining that his behaviour was not appropriate. This black man used to come to our fellowship with the Romanians because he liked to listen to how we sang and praised the Name of God. I reminded him that Jesus taught us in His Word that we should not fight with anyone, and that we are to love all people and be humble. The Spirit of God worked in that prisoner's heart and the conflict, which seemed endless, was settled and everything went back to normal.

Who do you think it was that was very, very angry with me for settling the dispute? None other than my 'friend' the Yugoslavian! He made a gesture with his big finger at his throat, and went back into his cell, slamming the door.

At dinner, I was with the recipient for tea. Each one of the 100 prisoners descended, one by one, to the table on the ground floor. When it was the turn of the prisoners on the first floor to come down, I saw that the Yugoslavian had a knife in his hand under his right sleeve. I thought immediately that he wanted to attack me, and so I started praying, and at the same time, I was ready to defend myself. When he came to take his cup of tea, he did not say a word, and passed by without doing anything. As he went up the steps to go to his cell, when he was near me, he dropped the knife which was hidden in his sleeve. I called to him, telling him that he had dropped the knife, and he turned to me and quite furiously picked up the knife. He came close to me and very smoothly touched my throat with it, telling me in German that he would kill me. To my own surprise, and that of my colleagues who were witnesses, I did not do anything. I smiled and let him go.

After this incident, I went to the director of our section, and told him in detail about the behaviour of this prisoner, who broke the rules and went beyond any limit in his relationship with the other prisoners and especially with myself. To my surprise, the director told me to bring him down a peg or two and give him a good beating.

Feeling encouraged by the director, the thought of revenge started to grow in my heart. Every day I was looking for the right opportunity to carry out my plan, and when the day came, I descended from my cell, determined to accomplish it. I was planning to get into this man's cell and teach him a lesson. This man was inferior to me in every way, but while I was going down the steps, the Spirit of God spoke directly to my heart, quoting Matthew 5:39-48. I froze!

I turned around and went back to my cell, throwing myself down on the ground, and praying for God's forgiveness. I was regretting the thoughts of revenge, and I was regretting that I wanted to do something against God.

I do not remember how long I spent in prayer, but I remember that I asked God what I should do. In my heart, I felt that the Spirit of God was exhorting me to do good to this Yugoslavian prisoner, and to pray for him. I knew that I could give him white bread, because

I shared the surplus with whom I wanted, but I had not given him any because I did not like him and because he did not respect me. I was convinced in my heart that God was urging me to do good to my enemy, because this was the way I could fulfill the words in Romans 12:20: '... *If your enemy is hungry, feed him; if he is thirsty, give him something to drink. In doing this, you will heap burning coals on his head.*'

I stood up, determined to do what the Bible said. I was ready to do everything God had put on my heart. So, the next day, for breakfast, I handed this man a piece of white bread. He took it, cursed me and slammed the door. I did not like this very much, but I was determined to continue the 'fight' with the armour of the Spirit and of the Word of God.

The guard that was with me signaled me in a way that meant: 'Go into his cell and bring him down a level.' I moved my head in such a way that meant I did not care anymore. At lunch I gave him the best portion, but again he looked at me with contempt, smiling in a mocking way.

I also met the Yugoslavian in the gym and I decided to help him, placing weights on the strength bar. Day after day, I humbled myself before God, and everything I did was according to the word of the scriptures: '*Whatever you do, work at it with all your heart, as working for the Lord, not for human masters* (Colossians 3:23).'

I don't know how long it had been since I started to do my best to show kindness to this Yugoslavian, trying to show him goodness...but I started to see with my own eyes how, little by little, this man's behaviour towards me changed day after day. He no longer showed contempt; he did not speak dirty language to me; and the day came when he even thanked me for the food I had given him. I was so happy seeing all that God was doing! I was happy that God had not allowed me to capture my heart with the feelings I had for this man at the outset.

The victory that filled my heart with thanks towards God came one evening when I was talking with some Romanians. When I turned my head to the Yugoslavian's cell, I saw him waving at me – he wanted me to go to him. I left the people I was talking to and went into his cell. I had heard it was his last day in prison, as he was going to be released the following day. As I got closer he stretched out his hand and said: 'Please forgive me for everything I did to you! I know why you did all that you did for me...' He had heard from a fellow citizen that I was a Christian and that I served the Lord Jesus Christ. When I heard these words, my heart was flooded with great joy. I was victorious through the One who loved and loves me so much! I was giving thanks to the Lord that, in prison, I was able to fulfil the word that is written in the Epistle to the Romans:

Do not repay anyone evil for evil. Be careful to do what is right in the eyes of everyone. If it is possible, as far as it depends on you, live at peace with everyone. Do not take revenge, my dear friends, but leave room for God's wrath, for it is written: 'It is mine to avenge; I will repay,' says the Lord... Do not be overcome by evil, but overcome evil with good. -Romans 12:17-19, 21

I was so happy that God had helped me to be one of his witnesses in that place! The Lord Jesus exhorts us through His Word, in Matthew 5:48: *'Be perfect, therefore, as your heavenly Father is perfect.*' When the man who trusts God loves, he is mature and complete, because God loves all people. When the one who is a born-again Christian forgives, he is mature and complete, because God forgives. I was happy, and I praised God for the 'exam' that I had passed, with help and power that I had received from Him.

Many people do not want to follow the Saviour Jesus, and do not want to repent of their sins, because the devil deceives them, saying: 'You cannot do this or that...'. Christ did not tell anyone in what condition they need to be to follow Him. He just said: *'He who wants to follow Me...'*. If you want to do God's will, it is God who works in you to will and to act in order to fulfil His good purpose.

When the Lord ascended to heaven, He made a wonderful promise: He promised His disciples that He would not leave them alone, but would send them the Holy Spirit, who would uncover everything the Father has, and that He would guide them into all truth. Glory to God for this extraordinary promise! The born-again Christian has the Holy Spirit as a guide on earth. How wonderful! Praise the Lord!

That night, when I went back to my cell, I was so happy! The Lord was magnified, and the evil one was put to shame. When I reached my cell, I knelt and praised God for the power He had given me to not put His Name to shame. The guards and prisoners all knew I could harm the Yugoslavian, and their respect for me was even greater now, due to the actions they had seen.

Anytime a fight arose, those who were involved came to me for advice and asked me to intervene. There was so much joy when I assisted them, with God's help, to reconcile and solve their misunderstandings. The guards were happy that in Haus IV, riots, fights, and misunderstandings were fewer and fewer, to the point (with just a few exceptions) of almost stopping. Everything was because of God, who was with me in all I did, and blessed me; and then through me, He blessed those around me!

Chapter 14

The days passed by and my thoughts were directed more and more to my second trial. I knew that the police in Bremen, where I did the first robbery, could not just give up on my trial. A year and six months had passed since I was imprisoned, and it was so hard for me to think about a new sentence, not knowing when I would return to the person I loved and cherished.

There were two Moldovans from Kishinev who came to listen to the Word of God anytime I had the opportunity to meet with the prisoners. One was named Alexandru, and the other was Ionel, and they had both come to Germany wanting to get rich. When we met in the cell for discussions, Alexandru listened very carefully to the Word of God. He did not say anything and he did not ask anything. Ionel would say a few words or ask a question, but Alexandru seemed dumb. He had come to Germany and had surrendered to the German authorities under a false name. Many Moldovans were doing that because, if the German authorities could not discover their true identity, they were forced to release them and provide work and lodging for them. And taking into account that the authorities in Kishinev did not cooperate with the German authorities, there was little chance of discovering their true identities. The Moldovans agreed to spend a year, or a year and a half, in prison; and then they could stay in Germany legally, according to the legislation at that time.

One morning, I saw Alexandru standing in front of my cell door. He was happy and a smile shone on his face: 'Last night I became a child of God and I surrendered my life to Him!' Alexandru exclaimed. 'What happened?' I asked.

He told me that he'd had a dream the night before. In his dream, it seemed that an unseen force was pushing him towards a deep black hole. No matter how hard he tried to oppose it, he could not stop his sliding towards that black hole. Suddenly, he started shouting for God's help. More than that, he shouted to the Lord and asked Him: 'Lord, what shall I do?' Then he heard a voice that said: 'Alexandru, you must repent and believe in Jesus Christ!' When he heard these words, he opened his eyes, looked around and stayed still for a few seconds. He got up from his bed, knelt and said: 'Lord Jesus, I surrender my whole life to You, and starting from today, I want to follow You and love You with all my heart!' After he said these words, his heart was flooded with a joy that he had never experienced before. He could hardly wait for the cell doors to open to tell me about this change in his life.

I looked at Alexandru with much joy, because I had experienced, a few months before, the same kind of joy that he was experiencing now. I hugged him, and we knelt together in my cell and thanked God with all our hearts.

The two Moldovans became part of the team I was leading, and we worked together in everything that was needed there. The director of the section was very pleased with all we were doing. He was pleased with the cleanliness, he was pleased with the fact that there was peace among us, and he was pleased that prisoners were no longer creating problems. In order to show his appreciation he bought a big cake and cookies for us. This had never happened before in that prison. I knew, by the way we were treated, that God's love was poured abundantly on that place, and I was convinced that God had granted me favour in the presence of these people.

The leadership of Haus IV at some point organised a football championship, which ended with a real banquet. They served grilled hot dogs, steaks, soda and cookies. This had never happened before either! God was blessing that place in an amazing way, and I cannot express in words the kindness and grace that God poured over Haus IV!

Everybody in that section, both the guards and the prisoners, knew that I was a Christian and that I served God with all my heart. They all respected me and loved me dearly, and all this was possible because of the grace of God, to whom I owed all the blessings in my life.

One day, Alexandru came to share a problem that bothered him; it was about the false name he had declared when he got into prison. He asked me what he should do next. I looked at him for a second or two, and because I knew it was a delicate issue, I did not rush to tell him what to do. I asked him if he believed, with all his heart, that God is Light. He said yes. Then I told him that all the people who want to live in the light must speak the truth from the heart. He looked at me and said that if he admitted the truth, he would be expelled to Kishinev, which he really did not want.

He told me that his mother was poor and sick and his heart's desire was to help her, and so he totally rejected what I had suggested. He turned his back and left my cell. I felt sorry for him and I was trying to understand him, but I could not possibly tell him that God agreed with the lie in which he was living.

I continued to pray for Alexandru. In the days that followed, he stopped talking with me, and he also stopped joining our meetings where we praised God and read from His Word. I was sorry for what was happening, but I continued to trust God, being fully convinced of the rightness of my advice to Alexandru.

After two weeks, Alexandru came to my cell again. He was downcast, head bowed down and very sad. He told me that, after he'd left my cell, he'd made the decision not to join our spiritual meetings that he had attended before. This was because he was upset with my advice to tell the truth, and he was scared of the consequences. What was worse, though, was the fact that at that point, when I gave him the advice, he lost his peace, joy and hope. I asked him what his intentions for the future were, and to my surprise, he said he wanted to declare his real name. 'Well done, I am glad you have accepted my advice,' I said to him. He looked me in the eye, his face shone, and he said firmly: 'I want to live in the light, to speak out the truth in any circumstance of my life, so that God can rejoice in me.'

The next day I went with him to the Social Department, where the clerk (a lady) could not believe her ears when we told her the reason we were there. I was there as a translator, as Alexandru did not speak German, and now I had learned some of the language.

The lady was confused and asked the Moldovan what made him admit to the truth so suddenly. When I told her that the reason was because Alexandru had become a Christian, and he wanted to give his real name, she looked at us even more amazed.

It was only normal that she did not understand, because she was not a born-again soul, and Jesus was not the Master of her life. That was why she dressed with little modesty, tempting the prisoners. She even enjoyed being a temptation and being admired. I understood what was happening, because when the Holy Spirit regenerates you and brings you to life together with Christ, you start seeing things differently than you did before. In the Epistle to the Ephesians, the Apostle Paul describes this truth (Ephesians 2:1-5).

After Alexandru had revealed his true identity we wanted to leave the room, but the clerk stopped us and expressed her desire to help Alexandru. She gave him an address he could write to and she told him that the people at that address could decide to expel him to Moldova, or give him the right to stay in Germany. When we left the office, the lady told us not to tell anyone about the address she'd given Alexandru.

We went to my cell and Alexandru asked me: 'So, what are we going to do now?' I answered: 'We're going to start writing a letter.' Alexandru did not know what we should write to the authorities that would help them to decide whether he could stay in Germany, or whether he would be forced to go back to Moldova; but we were determined to tell the truth. After we wrote a few lines, we marked them with a comma, and then we explained the reason why Alexandru was determined to declare his true identity. We sealed the envelope, prayed and sent it to the address we had been given.

In the evening, I was thinking about the absolutely unexpected reaction of the lady from the Social Department; it was so obvious and clear to me that it was God's hand. Surely God had a plan for Alexandru!

The next day, Alexandru had peace in his heart again, and he attended our gatherings to rejoice together in the goodness of God. Alexandru and I had so many reasons to thank God for the wonderful way in which He had worked in our lives.

Not long after this happy situation in Alexandru's life, one of the guards handed me a letter from the German DA. Because I was not so good at reading legal terms, I handed the letter to one of the guards, the oldest among them, to read it for me and to explain what the authorities required of me. While he was reading, I saw his amazement; he was looking at me and again seemed very amazed. As I could not stand this tension any more, I asked him to tell me what the letter said. Finally, after reading everything that was written, he told me the German DA said **that I was no longer held accountable for the first robbery, and that I was going to be sent to Romania**.

Totally amazed at what I heard, I could not believe my ears; I was looking both at the guard and at the letter, and I said to the guard in a harsh tone of voice not to mock me. Seeing that I did not believe him, he gave me the letter, turned around and left.

I was so excited by this news that I went to a different guard; after this one read the letter, he told me exactly what the first had already told me! Overwhelmed by the astonishing news, I went back to my cell and, filled with joy, I fell to my knees and thanked God for the wonderful way in which He was working in this area of my life. Truly, God had performed another miracle for me. I shared the news with the other Romanians, and we all praised God.

It was truly something extraordinary. Suddenly, I thought of my beautiful wife...

That week I phoned Mirela and told her that I was going to be home very soon. We were both so excited.

Chapter 15

It was July 1995. It had been almost a month since I'd received that letter from the DA, where it said that I was no longer held accountable for the first robbery in Bremen, but nothing had changed in my situation. If the words written in that letter were true – I was now mistrusting the translation of my letter by the two guards – the German authorities should have been preparing my expulsion from the country. No-one seemed to be doing anything in this respect. I started to be concerned, and an unusual restlessness captured my heart – my peace was gone, and so many thoughts were bombarding my mind.

On one of the following days, I took the letter and I went to the director of our section; I showed it to him and I told him what the two guards had told me. The director took the letter, read it, looked at me inquiringly and exclaimed: 'Something is not right!' He reached into one of the drawers in his desk and took out a letter which said that, on 5th September, I was going to be moved to a penitentiary in Bremen, where a trial was going to take place for my first robbery.

Suddenly I felt that my strength was fading away and I could hardly stand. I asked him to confirm once again what he had told me and he did, assuring me that this was how things were.

I left the director's office staggering around like a drunken man. When I reached my cell I hit the locker next to the door very hard, I was so furious at what the director had just told me! I could not believe my ears! In my head, all my thoughts were confused; everything crumbled down around me... I started shouting at God, holding Him accountable for what was happening. That day I dared to argue with my Creator! I could no longer understand what was going on... What was I going to tell my dear wife? That I was going to spend another two, three, or four years in prison? It was too much! The other prisoners found out the news I had received.

That day, my soul was crushed and I did not want to leave my cell. I told the others to take care of all the chores, food and the rest. I did not want to speak to or see anyone and I was like that for a week! All of Haus IV was sad because of me. Cheerfulness was buried, and when I had lunch with my team, no one said anything. I had no words left. I had all kinds of thoughts in my mind telling me I had to spend many more years in prison. Everything in me collapsed slowly and surely. I had no power to endure more years, far from the one I loved so much! I found no pleasure in reading my Bible; I was no longer praying...this hit nearly overwhelmed me!

A few more days had passed by when, while having lunch with my team of Romanians and Moldovans, I heard a voice inside me saying: 'Lift up your eyes and look around you; look how much sadness you have brought to those around you. Have you forgotten that, for your sake, I had an innocent man imprisoned for eight months? What would happen if you found out that there is a soul to be saved in the prison where you have to go? What shall I do? Send another innocent Romanian to spend a few months in prison to save that soul that cries for help?'

The moment I heard those words so clearly in my heart, I lifted up my eyes and I told those who were eating with me: 'What is with this sadness over you? The same way an innocent man spent eight months in prison to share the gospel with me, maybe there is a soul that needs salvation in the penitentiary where I am going... What should God do? Take another innocent man, lock him up and send him to share the good news of salvation with that man?'

Right after saying these words, the peace that comes from God flooded my whole being again, and cheerfulness and laughter came back to everybody's face.

On 3rd September I was on my way to the penitentiary in Bremen. On 5th September I had the first hearing in court. The trial should have lasted five days, but it lasted thirty days! It was a significant case, and due to the fact that there was not enough evidence, many people were summoned for hearings and more evidence was gathered.

The day I arrived in Bremen I asked if there were any Romanians. It was confirmed that there were three Romanians, for which I was very glad, and I tried to meet them. I went to the cell where the three Romanians were, and I noticed there was a New Testament on their table. I began a conversation with them that focused on God, and two of them seemed very pleased to hear someone talking with them about God. The third, who stayed in bed watching TV, was asking hostile questions. It was clear that this young man (he was only 20) from Bacau did not have any interest in hearing about God.

I told the other two Romanians, who were interested in listening to the Word of God, that the next meeting should be in my cell, and so that is exactly what happened. The next day the two Romanians were in my cell and I shared from my heart how God had changed my life in the penitentiary in Braunschweig – and I also shared about the need for the salvation of one's soul. After we'd talked for a few hours, they left for their cell.

The next day, as I was walking, I was surprised to see that the two Romanians who had seemed interested in the gospel preferred the company of other prisoners. I was sad in my heart and I was praying to the Lord to show me the soul He had told me needed salvation.

The same day, I heard from my cell someone speaking broken German in front of my door. The door opened and Ionel from Bacau, who had teased me when I shared from the Bible, came in. As he was standing in the door, he asked me if I had fought with Daniel Dancuţă in 1991, at the Senior National Championships. My answer was yes, and he told me he had watched that match on TV. He was amazed, and surprised, that I had repented; in his understanding, it was only lowly people and fools who repented.

I did not judge him harshly, because I myself had understood this word wrongly and I had also judged those who were called *pocăiţi*. I asked him to take a seat, and in a few hours, I shared the full Gospel, summarising the most important aspects.

Very surprised at what he had heard, Ionel stood

up and told me he wanted to repent. I thought he was joking and was mocking repentance. Then, suspecting that he was not serious, I warned him by saying that turning to God was not a game. I told him that God is love, but he is also a burning fire. After I'd warned him again that he should not play with God, and that the salvation of one's soul is not a game, Ionel stood up and left the cell, made very sad by all my threatening warnings.

After he left, I had a feeling of regret and fear that I had scared him and that, by talking to him the way I did, it was not very likely that Ionel would still want to repent. That is why, in the evening, I prayed for him and I asked for a sign from God.

I asked God, if Ionel was the soul He had told me about through the Holy Spirit, to bring him back to my cell the next day, without my asking him to do so. If he came, I was ready before God not to be so unwise anymore, like I was that day, and I would not scare him anymore. More than that, I would not speak about anything but God's kindness and love! If he was the one indeed, then I asked God to put it on Ionel's heart to speak to me more about his salvation.

The next day, Ionel came to me in my cell without my asking him to do so. He was very serious, and was no longer joking. I asked him many questions, rambling about his life in Bacau and many other topics that had nothing to do with God. Ionel asked me to keep quiet and to listen to him. 'Last night' – he began his confession – 'I did not sleep at all. I thought that if I did not repent I would go to hell, and hell is a place of torment and pain. All night I had all these thoughts going through my mind. I came here just to hear you speaking about God and nothing else, because I want to repent and believe in Jesus, the Saviour, with all my heart!'

When I heard him speaking I was fully convinced, due to the sign I had asked from God, that Ionel was the soul that the Spirit of God had told me about in the penitentiary in Wolfenbuttel. I gladly shared with him about Jesus' sacrifice, and the blessings a man receives when he turns to God. These were uplifting moments together with Ionel, and when I finished talking, we both knelt and we prayed to God that He would radically change Ionel's life. I was glad to hear him praying and entrusting his life into the hands of God. When we stood up, Ionel removed his gold earring from one of his ears and threw it in the toilet. We hugged and Ionel went back to his cell, which was above my cell.

I had a long and difficult trial. During the thirty days of the trial, I received a letter that came from outside the penitentiary, from an unknown address. When I opened the envelope and started to read the letter, my eyes filled with tears; it was from Alexandru. After I left he had received an answer from the address where we had sent his letter telling the truth about himself. The German authorities had decided to let him go free, and offered him both work and lodging – it was great news and a miracle from God! Humanly speaking, Alexandru's chances were zero, but when you decide to honour God and live in the light, God honours you in turn and His blessing comes down on you. This is what happened with Alexandru, who had decided to tell the truth. God was making my trial easier through the joy I had from Alexandru and Ionel. Ionel was making remarkable spiritual progress, walking in the way of faith and repentance in a very serious way. He was very interested, and was asking many questions, and I was rejoicing with him every day over all that God was revealing to us from His Word.

After a month, my trial was over. Just as God had rewarded Gigi Sabău with a sum of money, with which the German authorities repaid him for being in prison as he was not guilty of anything, my reward (for Ionel) was a suspended sentence. The court decided to end my sentence and send me back to Romania. If I were ever to come back to Germany, then I would have one year and three months left to serve, in addition to a new sentence, if I did something wrong.

I had no words with which to thank God. Even though the people in Wolfenbuttel had 'encouraged' me by saying that I was going to receive at least five more years, the God in whom I put my trust and whom I serve decided that I should be sent home!

When I went back to Wolfenbuttel and told them my sentence, almost no one believed me. Most of my cellmates from Wolfenbuttel thought I was joking and hiding the truth. I was no longer interested in what they were saying; my thoughts were towards my lovely wife. After two very long years we were going to see each other again!

Chapter 16

On 5th December 1995 I was leaving Wolfenbuttel for Romania. There was great sadness among those in Haus IV when I left, and even the guards found it difficult to say goodbye to me! God had changed so many things in my life, and this was noticed even by the people who had to guard us, as it would be hard for them to find a prisoner like me in the near future. Of course, I owed everything to God; He deserves all the praise, thanks and worship.

I was at the Düsseldorf airport, waiting for my plane to Romania to come. It was a cold winter, and there was a great deal of snow in Bucharest. We waited a long time at the Düsseldorf airport, and then the policemen who were accompanying us at the airport gave us news that almost stopped my heart! We had to go back to the penitentiaries we came from, because the airport in Bucharest was covered in heaps of snow, and the plane we were waiting for could not take off.

It was such devastating news!!

All the time I was waiting at the Düsseldorf airport, I was thinking that I would see Mirela, my beloved wife, that very night. I had left Wolfenbuttel on Monday, stayed overnight in a different penitentiary where there were other Romanians who were going to Romania, and on Wednesday we'd reached Düsseldorf. Now, as we were supposed to go back, we had to follow the same route again – a night in the Hanovra Penitentiary, and then, Thursday night, I was back in Wolfenbuttel, where I had spent a year. I was thinking about what the people there would say; what would their faces show when they saw me there again so soon?

Thursday evening, after a long and exhausting journey, I reached Haus IV at Wolfenbuttel. It was late at night and the prisoners were already in their cells, so they would not know that I was back. My former cell was still empty, and so I asked the guards to assign me to the same cell – and I also asked them if it was possible for me to serve breakfast the next day. Like any Romanian, when in hard times, I was going to make the best of a bad bargain! The next day, dressed in a white robe, I was yelling in the hallways: 'Good morning, boys, here is your breakfast!'

It is hard to describe what happened that morning. Hearing my voice, the prisoners dashed to the cell doors, exclaiming: 'This is impossible, it is not true! It cannot be Vasile Tofan!' We had such a laugh that morning. When most of the prisoners in Haus IV were at their cell doors, I waved my hand and said: 'My dear friends, seeing how sad you were when I left, I decided to come back and stay with you to the end!' You can imagine what happened next! Some were whistling, others were yelling, some were tapping on the railing there was a real uproar. After we had a good laugh, everything went back to normal. I had to spend another week there before I went back to the Düsseldorf airport. When I left, everyone said they were waiting for me to come back soon. Even though this was a good joke, I was asking myself if, this time, the plane would come and pick us up in good weather.

Everything went well, and on 13th December, I arrived at the airport in Bucharest. Here, one of the Romanians who had spent two or three months at Wolfenbuttel was waiting for me. When he was released from prison, due to the fact that I had helped him to get out of his bad state of spirit when he was in Haus IV, he had promised he would come to the airport to pick me up. To my great joy, this man (originally from Ploiesti) kept his word and came to the airport in Bucharest... where my faith was going to be put to the test again.

I had two suitcases, a typewriter and a stereo, and one of the Romanians who had travelled with me offered to help with my luggage. He had been in a different penitentiary.

After the policemen checked our passports at the airport, I reached the point where luggage was brought in from the plane, but I could only see one bag and the stereo. The other bag and the typewriter were not there – the conveyer belt stopped, but my other luggage was still missing. I addressed one of the employees and told him about the incident. He indicated the route for the luggage that ended up in a storage room where my other belongings would be, and he encouraged me to go there to look for it. I also took the other Romanian with me, to find them more quickly. While we were looking for the luggage I discovered it: the bag and the typewriter. At that moment the other Romanian asked me: 'Is this your luggage?' I thought he was asking me about my belongings that I had just found – not seeing the huge suitcase in his hand – and I answered in the affirmative.

I took the typewriter, which was packed in a box, and the bag. Even though I noticed that the other man had a bag that was not mine, I was so happy to have found my luggage that I did not pay any attention to that bag and I did not ask him whose it was. Going upstairs, the clerk looked at me and asked: 'Are you sure all this is your luggage?' Thinking that he was asking just about my bags, I answered affirmatively with total conviction.

We took all the bags and went to the exit of the airport. We also had the big bag with us that my colleague had taken from the storage area, thinking it was mine. Close to the exit we encountered the man who had come to wait for me as he had promised; we hugged and were about to leave the airport when a few policemen came to us. They stopped us and asked us what was in our bags. I do not know what they wanted, but the man from Ploiesti who had come to wait for me rebuked them a little and they let us go.

When we reached the car that belonged to the man from Ploiesti, I put all my bags in the trunk. There was just one bag left that did not belong to me. I asked whose it was and why it was there. The man who had helped me with my belongings asked me why I asked such questions. He said: 'Did I not ask you in the storage room if this is your luggage, and you said yes?' At that moment, I realised that the evil one had blinded our minds, so that we did not realise what we were doing. Immediately, I decided to take the suitcase back, but the one who had taken it did not want to take it back. I told them that, in that moment, we were guilty of theft. Eventually we went back with the baggage.

When we entered the airport again, we met the same

police crew that had stopped us on our way out. They asked us what the problem was, and we said we wanted to take this bag back from where we took it, because we realised we had made a mistake. When they heard us, the policemen looked at us as if we were aliens! They said something to their colleagues, but they used coded language, and in a few minutes we were surrounded by several policemen. We were taken to a room, and the bag was X-rayed. I heard someone reporting from the room with the bag: 'There is no explosive here, boss!' Then I realised that we were being mistaken for terrorists who were planning an attack. I could not believe the situation we were unwittingly in! Once they were convinced there were no explosives in the bag, one of the policemen told me to take the bag back to the storage room where my colleague had taken it by mistake. When all this was over, those people thanked me for my honesty and they let me go. Confused because of all these events, I omitted to let them know the real reason why I'd given them back the bag… I was sorry I had not told them that the Lord had changed my heart and life, and that this was the true reason why I'd handed this bag back to where it belonged, because it was not mine.

When we reached the Ploiesti man's car, we set out for Ploiesti, but we travelled in silence, each one of us thinking about what had just happened. I did not know how to thank God enough for keeping me safe from the catastrophe that had almost fallen on me. I was thinking that we could have encountered the owner of the bag, or he could have seen us with it… What would we have told him to prove that we were not planning to steal it? Who would have believed us? We would be the main suspects, because we were coming from a prison in Germany where we had done time for robbery.

I thanked God with all my heart for watching over me. This was a test that God had allowed so that my faithfulness to Him could be tested. Blessed be God, I passed it with flying colours...and this was possible only because of His grace!

We reached Ploiesti late at night; there was no train at that hour going to Galati and I had to wait until the next morning, when a fast train from Bucharest would pass through Ploiesti on the way to Galati. Gigi, from Onești, remained at the train station in Ploiesti, hoping that he would find a way to get home, but I went to the apartment of this man who had waited for me at the airport. After I met his wife, I asked for permission to call my wife, whom I had not called in four months. They gladly allowed me to use their phone. When I heard Mirela's voice, a thrill went through my body and an overwhelming excitement came over me. She was at home, and in just a few hours, we were going to be together again.

Surprised to hear my voice, with an inquiring tone, she asked: 'Where are you?' I told her I was in Romania, in Ploiesti, where I was staying overnight at one of my acquaintances, and that I was using his phone. She would not believe my words, and so I told her to write down the number of the phone I was using and to call me back. She did, and only then did she believe me.

After calling Mirela, fully convinced that in a few hours I was going to see my dear ones, first Mirela and then the rest, I talked about the Bible with this man and his wife. I knew it would be hard for me to sleep with all this excitement, so I stayed up all night.

I had met this man, my host, a few months earlier at the penitentiary in Wolfenbuttel. He was a man with a solid university education, in whom one would expect to see a healthy and uncompromising moral life, but in spite of these expectations, he went to the West and got involved in some scams. As the Romanian proverb says, 'the pitcher goes often to the well, but is broken at last'. The German police eventually managed to catch him in the act, and he was locked up.

During his time in prison, my behaviour caught his attention. I took advantage of his obvious interest and explained to him where and how I got this power to behave differently from the other Romanians imprisoned there. In other words, I shared the gospel with him, emphasising the love of our Lord Jesus Christ. He is the only One in whom we can believe for our salvation, which means we can then be forgiven of any sin committed, and we are able to live a new life, a radically changed life, with the power to be different and to live differently, which we receive from Him through the Holy Spirit.

After spending a few months together we said goodbye, as he was released and sent back to Romania. There he forgot all the things I had shared with him, living his life like he used to live before being imprisoned. The seed of the Word of God fell among thorns, as it is written in the Parable of the Sower in Luke 8:14: *'The seed that fell among thorns stands for those who hear, but as they go on their way they are choked by life's worries, riches and pleasures, and they do not mature.'*

Early in the morning, I said goodbye to my host, thanking him for having hosted me that night, and I wished him the best. I also told him to think about the things I had talked to him about from the scriptures during the time that we were together, both in Wolfenbuttel prison and in his house.

When I reached the train station I bought a ticket and very excitedly got on the train; I was home, in Romania, and I was on my way to Galati, the city I left to go to Western Europe, where I thought I would be somebody and where I would receive help to come back an accomplished man, a rich man. Well, I had not come back a rich man, but my experience in Germany had dramatically changed my entire life. The former Vasile Tofan, who had left to conquer the world, remained in the penitentiary in Braunschweig; he'd 'died' there, and now I was a totally changed man, a man with new thinking, renewed by the Word of God and by the Holy Spirit!

All the way to Galati, I thought about the time spent in the penitentiary, and about the wonderful way in which God had blessed me. As I was thinking about my wonderful experience with God, and praising Him in my heart, the train got very close to Galati. I saw, from the window, the impressive viaduct that links the city to the iron and steel plant.

I was overwhelmed with excitement, especially once the train got out of the tunnel; little by little we reached the train station. I stood up quickly, took my bags, and when the train stopped, I opened the door and saw Mirela, my beloved wife! She had not changed a bit; the same charming eyes, the same long black hair, the same slender body...

I got out and we hugged for a long time. We had been apart for two years and a month, but now we were back together! We could hardly stop crying, Mirela and myself! We took a taxi from the train station and we went to my in-laws' house in Micro 13B. When I entered the house, my sister-in-law said that my face was shining! I was back after two years, and in that time, God had changed my whole being.

The celebration of the Birth of the Lord was getting closer. The days that were left before this great celebration in the Christian world, and then the New Year, passed so quickly! We were so happy that we hardly noticed how the days went by.

I was eager to see the other members of my family, so together with Mirela, I took the first trip to Brasov to visit my older brother, Milică, my nephews and nieces, and my sister-in-law, Viorica. From Brasov, we went to Piatra Neamț, where most of my family lived: my parents, my middle brother Dan, and Lăcrămioara, the youngest in the family. We spent the winter holidays there.

My family and my relatives could hardly believe that I was no longer the one I used to be. They thought I was pretending. I could understand this very well, because none of them were familiar with the Holy Scriptures, the Word of Life that had dramatically and radically changed my life. Their faith was formal, like most people's. They only had rituals that they followed and that was all. They knew nothing of being born again; and they knew nothing about the celebration they kept, which was more according to custom and human traditions than real spiritual truth.

I had long and serious discussions with them regarding my faith. It was hard for them to believe that the one who used to do stupid things was now talking about faith in God, the salvation of the soul, eternal life and many other blessings which are received by one's encountering Jesus, the Saviour.

I desired that all my family would repent as soon as possible, and I shared other fundamental topics with them from the Holy Scriptures such as the Kingdom of God, the forgiveness of sins through faith in the sacrifice of the Saviour, being born again, and so on, and so on...

I must admit that in my attempt to persuade them of these truths, I had discovered and encountered a lot of naivety when it came to the Bible. How could they believe so soon? Even Nicodemus, one of the Jewish leaders, could not understand when talking with Jesus. Jesus told Nicodemus: *'Very truly I tell you, no one can enter the kingdom of God unless they are born of water and the Spirit. Flesh gives birth to flesh, but the Spirit gives birth to spirit* (John 3:5-6).'

In order for man to understand that which comes from God, he needs to be born of the Spirit of God. This is how it is written in the Holy Scriptures.

Chapter 17

After the holidays we came back to Galati. I thanked God that on New Year's Eve I could be with my dear ones, and especially with my beloved wife.

I prayed every day to God for Mirela to understand that she needed forgiveness and salvation. She had been a very moral person before our marriage, and that is why she could not understand why she needed to repent. She kept telling me that she had not killed anybody, she did not steal, she did not commit immoral acts, and so she did not consider herself a sinful woman. I showed her what the scriptures say in Romans 3:23: 'For all have sinned and fall short of the glory of God.' I had many heated discussions with her on this matter. One day she threatened me with divorce if I did not let her live her life peacefully – that persuaded me to pray more fervently for her. Even though she would sometimes brutally reject me, I decided to trust the Lord with all my heart and wait patiently until God convinced her of her sins and the need for forgiveness and salvation. I decided to preach the gospel with my life and in my everyday actions.

It seemed as if everything was new in Galați. Most people in my hometown had heard that I was back from Germany, and there were different stories going around about me. My old colleagues could not understand the change in me. They had heard that I had repented, but this word, in their minds, had the same derogatory and negative connotations that I'd had not long ago. I tried to explain to them what had happened to me, but most of them shrugged their shoulders or nodded their heads, a sign that meant I had gone crazy. I had become an uncomfortable person for them to be with because I no longer used the bad language that I once had, and I had no pleasure in going to the restaurants I used to visit, and my former friends could not understand my new lifestyle.

Obviously I was eager to get to my former workplace to see my employer, Ionel Florea. This man, who was educated, a smart guy, quickly acknowledged the change in me. I was a new man; the old Vasile Tofan was dead.

I had many talks with him about faith and I exhorted him, as I did with the rest of my acquaintances, to read the Holy Scriptures. We met often, and our talks were mainly on spiritual topics. It seemed that my former boss understood what I was explaining regarding the scriptures and true faith.

I was also happy to meet again with my old friend Laurențiu Gaftiuc, and I talked with him a lot about the Bible as well. One day as I was walking with him downtown we passed a construction site, and Laurențiu told me that a church of *pocăiți* was being built there. I wanted to get in touch with someone there, and I managed to get the phone number of Pastor Ovidiu Ghiță, the man who was supervising the work at the construction site.

The pastor invited me to attend the church services,

which were then being held in the old building, on
Balcescu Street. Brother Ovi, as the parishioners called
him, was happy to hear my testimony and how I came
to turn to God. In the Bible it says that when a man
is born again, he becomes a member of the Body of
Christ, which is the Church, and from now on I needed
to take my place there. The Church of Jesus Christ is
made up of born-again people, and this was the reason
I started regularly attending the church services held
in the building on Balcescu Street. I was so glad when
believers gathered in the church to praise the Name of
God in singing, prayer and listening to the Word. I was
delighted, seeing the unity among the believers, and
very quickly I felt I was a part of this wonderful family.

One day, Mirela came with me to a church service,
and she was delighted with everything she saw and
heard there. Shortly after, we both attended a service
where we got invited to the wedding of a couple from
the church. I was very glad to go with my lovely wife,
and around 11pm we left for home. We were so happy
to have attended this wedding and to have seen how it
all went! I left for home without being drunk, talking
dirty, or being bothered by any passersby. All these
things would have happened before I knew God.

Everything was so lovely at this wedding! The youth
sang songs to the glory of God, we talked openly and
warmly with the other guests, and no one broke the
'good manners' code. Mirela noticed that the people –
those with whom she talked – talked to her as if they
had known her for a long time. She was impressed with
everything she saw at this wedding.

I had a burning desire to get baptised, according to

the command of the Saviour Jesus, written in Mark 16:16. Baptism is the confession of a clean conscience before God, and through baptism, you confess shamelessly that you agree to die, together with Christ, to the sinful systems of this world, and you come into a new life together with Christ, who becomes your Saviour and Lord (Master). The same way that Jesus was not ashamed to die on the cross for the sins of the whole world, the faithful soul is not ashamed to declare, from his heart, his faith in God.

I know that most Romanians are ashamed to get baptised as adults, declaring that they were baptised as infants. But, in the same way you are judged by the Penal Code if you make a mistake towards society, God will judge the world according to the Holy Scriptures. In John 12:47-48, the Lord Jesus says: *'If anyone hears my words but does not keep them, I do not judge that person. For I did not come to judge the world, but to save the world. There is a judge for the one who rejects me and does not accept my words; the very words I have spoken will condemn them at the last day.'*

If you want to become a mathematician, you need to learn maths; if you want to become a doctor, you need to learn human physiology and anatomy; if you want to become a driver, you need to know the legislation and the road code. In the same way, if you want to become a Christian, you need to read and keep the words written in the Holy Scriptures. If the driver wants to retain his license and money in his pocket, he needs to obey the traffic rules. If a man wants to be happy, he needs to obey God. Everything that God asks of us is written in the Bible, the Book of Life.

On 5th May 1996 I obeyed God's command and got baptised. On this occasion, my former employer, Mr Ionel Florea, attended. I knew that he was aware of the truth regarding the life of faith; it was just because of shame, and the fact that some of his colleagues started talking behind his back, that he came to church only once in a while – and he was avoiding me.

In Jesus' time, Pilate, the Roman governor, totally understood that He was innocent, and yet, because of the crowds and for the fear of man and the desire to keep his position as governor, he yielded and condemned Jesus, the Lord of Life, to death.

The Word of God says that if you want to please men, you are an enemy of God. Of course I understood Mr Ionel Florea, but I think that, if he leaves this world without fulfilling God's command, then on that day God will have no compassion on him.

One of the reasons people refuse to fulfil the Word of God in their lives is embarrassment before their neighbours. But if you are ashamed of God in this life, there will come a time when He will be ashamed of you!

My old friends wanted to lure me into all kinds of places where God was not present. Their joy was a bottle of wine or beer, gossiping and mocking someone, and having immoral relationships with different women. When you are spiritually blind you cannot distinguish light from darkness, or life from death. Lies, fornication, gossip, hatred, bad jokes, envy, selfishness, dirty talk, do not seem out of the ordinary to you; more than that, you consider them normal. When God brings you to life together with Christ, all these disappear from your life and you see them as God sees them – as sinful habits, harming the soul and the inner man.

Repentance is a change to the way you think, a change of direction. It comes from the Greek term *metanoia*, which means a renewing of one's mind. Man, as long as he is alive, can repent. That is, he is able to change the way he thinks, renewing his mind; after he dies there is nothing else that can be done. This is God's command. In Acts 17:30 it says: *'In the past God overlooked such ignorance, but now he commands all people everywhere to repent. For he has set a day when he will judge the world with justice by the man he has appointed. He has given proof of this to everyone by raising him from the dead.'*

I have met so many people who have said they've repented; it's just that their lives showed the opposite. A good tree bears good fruit, and a bad tree bears bad fruit. You will know the people by their fruit, that is, by their deeds and by the way they live. No one can draw sweet and bitter water from the same well, and in the same way, no one can speak about God, and later talk dirty or lie. What is inside comes out: *'For the mouth speaks what the heart is full of* (Luke 6:45).' If God is in your heart, your mouth will speak about God; if not, you will speak out of what is in your heart.

I was very glad that Ionel from Bacau attended my baptism – he is the one who gave his life to God in Bremen. After my baptism, even more than before, I had a burning desire to tell others about the love of God, and so I prayed every day for this wish to be fulfilled. Then one Sunday, after the morning service, Pastor Ovidiu Ghiță took me, together with other believers, to the penitentiary in Galați. That day, some prisoners were brought into a classroom. When I saw them I was shocked: most of them were my old companions in having fun and worldly pleasures. I could hardly speak to them with more than a few words, because in my mind there was this thought that they would not accept anything I told them. Surely it would be hard for them to believe that I had changed, that I was a different Vasile Tofan.

I left the prison in Galați determined not to go there again to preach the gospel. None of those present there thought I was a genuine believer, and they all said I was pretending. How could I have convinced them? I had no idea how I should have gone about things and what I could have said to them to make them believe me.

Three years passed, and in 2000, a foundation in Constanța suggested that I become a missionary to penitentiaries. I was more mature, God had helped me to grow in my faith, so I accepted their suggestion. I was going to the penitentiary in Galați again (obviously as a missionary), and the moment I passed through the gate, I felt love and compassion for those who were locked in there. I knew and believed that the One who had changed my life, and helped me to be born again, could do the same for any prisoner there.

In the penitentiary in Brăila I met a soul who was there for the fourth time. When he was 19 he was arrested for the first time, and afterward he had three more arrests. I met him in the penitentiary's social room. I found out that his cellmates had convinced him to come, because he did not want to hear anything about *pocăiți*. He was one of the tough guys in the penitentiary.

The day he came to the penitentiary's social room,

God gave me grace and power to share the Word, which searched his heart and made him ask questions regarding his life. At the end of the meeting he came to me and asked for a Bible. That day, I had an extra Bible with me (besides my own Bible) so I gave him the book – but the moment he reached out to take it, I pulled it back. 'If you want to take this book, read it and then continue with your life like you have done so far, then go back to your cell,' I told him. 'This book is not for you. But if you want to take this book to read it and live out what is written in there, then take it, it is for you!' He stretched out his hand and took it.

In the days that followed I heard that, little by little, something was changing in this man's life, and I was happy to hear that his life was changing day by day and his cellmates could see it. After two years, in 2002, he was released from prison for the fourth time; but Gică Doru Ciornei came out of prison a born-again man. He was going out of the prison gate convinced that he would never go back there, because he was determined to live his life the way God showed us, written in His Word. When the right time came, he married a girl from the Republic of Moldova, and God has blessed them with two children. Doru has definitively turned his back on the life of crime, and today he is a man who serves God!

Chapter 18

When man comes into this world, he is born with a thirst that no one and nothing can quench, except for God. Being thirsty, man tries to quench his thirst by drinking from the 'wells' of this world, which the evil one, the enemy of the human soul and the enemy of God, brings to him: money, booze, immoral pleasures, sinful fun and so on. The more man drinks from these wells, he becomes thirstier and thirstier and more and more unhappy. The Lord Jesus came into this world so that the man who trusts in Him could be truly happy and fulfilled. The Saviour Jesus said: *'Let anyone who is thirsty come to me and drink. Whoever believes in me, as Scripture has said, rivers of living water will flow from within them...* (John 7:37-38).'

When you drink water from an external source, it is very possible that someone will cut off this source, and so you no longer have access to it for a while. But if you dig a well in your courtyard, no one can cut off the water, because it springs from your well, situated on your land. In the same way it is with a man who looks for external joy – there comes a time when someone can cut off or steal his joy. If your joy is money, your business can become unprofitable, you can be bankrupted, and then your joy is over. If your joy is in your pocket or the bank, it is possible that someone can put his hand into your pocket or steal from your bank account, and your joy is finished. But, if your joy is in the heart, having God as the Master of your life, well, no one can put his hand in your heart and steal your joy. The man who trusts in Jesus has joy after joy, because there is a spring in his heart that can never go dry. What a pity that so many people look for fulfilment, joy and happiness outside!

In 2001 I met a 20-year-old young man in the penitentiary in Galați, originally from Liești, a village in Galați County. When the police arrested him, a crowd of people gathered in front of the police station, asking the policemen to shoot him. I found out that he had terrorised the entire village and people had been avoiding him. After he had listened to my testimony and heard about the way I turned to God, Florin Dorosan asked for a Bible. I prayed for him, and I asked others to pray for him. From one meeting to another, I could see how God was changing the features of his face; from a dark, sin-distorted face, Florin started to have a shining face, with the help of the Holy Spirit and the Word of God. I was glad to hear that Florin was bearing fruit worthy of his repentance. I found out that he had destroyed a packet of cigarettes that his family had brought him (in prison, a packet of cigarettes is 'hard currency'). Florin was determined to live according to God's Word, and he knew that a cigarette destroys one's health and life. I praised God for how Florin was determined to live.

After four years and seven months in jail, Florin was released. I drove him to Liești, where his six brothers, parents and close relatives were waiting for him. When he went into the courtyard, there was a demijohn of wine to celebrate his return. Florin, with a Bible in his hand, told them that the one who once did a lot of bad things, the man they knew, had 'died' in prison. He told everybody that he had repented in prison and wanted to live a life pleasing to God. When they heard him talking, those present there thought that Florin had gone mad. How strangely people behave sometimes! If you no longer want to lie, steal, or commit antisocial acts, those around you think you are insane.

The days went by and Florin started sharing about his Master, who was ruling his life; and I was glad to hear that he went to those whom he had wronged and asked for forgiveness. One day he went to the police station to give a Bible to the people there, and the policeman who had arrested him and sent him to jail was on duty that day. Florin thanked him for sending him to prison. Amazed, the policeman confessed that in 15 years of work on the Force, no one had ever thanked him for such a thing. Later he found out why Florin thanked him: because he had discovered Jesus Christ in prison, the One who had changed his life.

Even though he was not expecting to ever get married, God blessed Florin with a woman from the neighbouring village, whom he married. Today they have three children, and Florin has definitely turned his back on a life of crime.

In Romanian prisons there are psychologists, educational programmes, and all sorts of means to help the prisoners leave their bad habits so they need never come back to prison and can straighten out their lives. In spite of these services, prisons become more and more populated and crowded. Why? Because worldly systems do not make a man a new person who has fundamentally changed. 'In order to change a man into a saint, grace needs to intervene; who doubts that proves that he neither knows what a saint is, nor a man (Blaise Pascal).'

Since the gospel entered the Romanian prisons, God has given new life to people, who later become useful and special. Why? Because the gospel is the power of God for the salvation of each one who believes. Jesus Christ did not come to earth to change someone's religion. Out of the question! He came so that man can be born again. He who is in Christ is a new creation.

Today people argue about religious topics. God is not religion; He is a Person, interested in you and in how you live your life. God loves you and wants to help you become like his Son: humble, loving, living in holiness, obeying the Heavenly Father in all things. How wonderful! In the Garden of Eden, God created man according to His image and likeness, but after he was deceived by Satan, man received the likeness of the evil one: proud, envious, mean, selfish, criminal minded... How good would it be for man to fear God and do what is pleasing and beautiful in His sight! Then we would no longer need to barricade ourselves behind our doors, we would no longer need sophisticated alarm systems and we would no longer need bodyguards.

We live in a world that ignores Him and fights heavily to remove God definitively from the equation of life. People love darkness more than light. Why did they crucify Jesus? No one could prove Him wrong of a sin or a filthy act. Nevertheless, they crucified Him.

He did good things for people, He raised people from the dead, He healed the blind and He even loved his enemies.

One Sunday morning I was at church in Galati, and after the service was over, a young lady approached me and asked me directly: 'How can you be so sure that there is a God, and how do you know that what you do is pleasing to Him?' I was a little confused, and my first thought was to send her to the pastor. The pastor – I said to myself – could answer her much better than I could. But suddenly I remembered the man who was blind from birth. We can find his story in the Gospel of John, chapter 9. I told that young lady that I had been blind, like the man in the story, but that now I could see. I was blind when I had called darkness light, lies truth and evil good; but then I ended up in prison, where I found a book that had helped me, through the Holy Spirit, to believe in Jesus, the Son of God. He taught me to name light, light; truth, truth; and good, good. I was blind, but now I could see! How wonderful it is to be a child of God! How wonderful it is to live in truth and light! Fear goes away.

After the fall of man, in the Garden of Eden, fear gripped man's whole being. Jesus came to relieve us from the fear of death, to save us, getting us out from under the slavery of sin. Any man who believes in Jesus becomes a free and a fearless man. People should only fear God, but, because they do not trust in Him, they fear their fellow man, they fear tomorrow, and they have many other fears too.

My older brother was a religious man, but did not have the faith that could save your soul. Every time

I went to visit him in Brașov, I had many talks and
debates with him about real faith. His desire was to
make his family as happy as possible, a wish that any
parent has. He has a daughter and a son and I told him
that, without God, he could not fulfil this objective. He
told me that he is faithful, but he did not know a single
verse from the Bible. It is as if I say I am a maths teacher,
but I have no idea what 1 + 1 is. I was astonished that
Milică, my older brother, could not understand what I
was telling him from the Holy Scriptures, even though
he was a learned man, a military man by career, in a
military unit in Râșnov. More than that, I was amazed
at his reluctance and the hostile attitude he had towards
me, even though I was speaking politely and with
clear arguments. When I came back from Germany, I
thought that my older brother would be the first to turn
to God, and believe with all his heart in the sacrifice
of the Saviour. I should not have been amazed at my
brother's reluctance, because Matthew 10:36 says: *'A
man's enemies will be the members of his own household'*.
Why is this? Because a man without God lives in the
dark and is spiritually blind.

On one occasion I met him in his apartment in Brașov.
I remember that, after a heated discussion, I stood up
from the chair where I was sitting and I told him: 'This
very moment I will kneel and say a prayer for you and
I believe, with all my heart, that if you have the courage
to say "Amen" at the end of it you will surely repent.'
My older brother got angry at my words; he insisted
that he would say 'Amen', but would never repent. The
next moment, I knelt and I lifted up my voice to God
in prayer. After I finished my prayer, I said 'Amen' and

I heard him say it too. I stood up and told him that 'Amen' meant 'So be it'.

Shortly after that my brother started reading the scripture (he had never read from it before), writing down in a notebook the verses he thought were important. I was happy about all that was happening, especially because of what is written in the second part of James 5:16: *'The prayer of a righteous person is powerful and effective'.* Those who have repented of their sins and believe with all their heart in Jesus are righteous through what the Saviour accomplished on the cross at Golgotha.

In 2004, he decided to obey God's command; but what brought much joy to my heart was the fact that my sister Lăcrămioara and my brother-in-law got baptised together with him. I was glad and I thanked God that I had the privilege to preach at this beautiful and extremely special celebration. After he got baptised, my brother dedicated his life totally to God, and today he is a servant of God, honouring and loving Him with all his heart.

A year later, in 2005, my mother and my middle brother Dan got baptised, and then my father got baptised in 2006. I had no words to thank God for the fact that my family was in His hand!

Then my beloved wife got baptised at the same time; she entered into a covenant with the Lord in 2005. Because she had been a moral woman – even before our marriage – and had not committed terrible sins, it was harder for her to understand that you do not need to be guilty of great sins to repent before God. A filthy thought, a lie, pride, envy – all these and many other things like these, however small, are sins because God is holy and lives in a light that no one can get near. If a man on earth could have lived without sinning, then Jesus would not have come to die. But, because all men have sinned and fallen short of the glory of God, His glorious sacrifice was necessary!

In Galaţi, the rumour that Vasile Tofan had repented spread with the speed of light and everyone was totally amazed at what they heard. If you speak with people regarding repentance, some of them admit and acknowledge that it is needed; but if you tell them that more is required of them than the simple recognition of this truth, that they must obey this command which the One who created the universe gave for all of us, then these people become reluctant and hesitant. Is it possible that Jesus the Saviour would have given us teaching that, when obeyed precisely, would bring someone shame, dishonour and humiliation? Certainly not! The Golden Verse of the Scriptures (John 3:16) says: *'For God so loved the world that he gave his one and only Son, that whoever believes in him shall not perish but have eternal life.'* If you truly believe that God gave His only begotten Son to die for all mankind out of love, then it is impossible to think that God would have asked something inhumane and despicable from us! The word *repentance* is a godly word, which came from the mouth of the One who came down from heaven. That means that what the Lord said to the people was to help them. The Devil is the one who perverted this godly word, inoculating people's minds with the idea that repentance is something despicable.

The Holy Scriptures say that the devil is the father

of lies, and that is why he has lied to mankind right from the very beginning. Throughout the years there have been important people who repented; that is, they turned from sins to God. Among them I can mention Christopher Columbus, Isaac Newton, Abraham Lincoln and many other important people in this world. Life without God is like a boat with no ferryman. Vasile Tofan, the one without God, ended up in prison at the age of 24, a moment when his life could have taken a tragic turn – if God had not had mercy on him. God saved my life, saved my marriage, restored my dignity; He has made me a new man, by birth from above, and given me a new nature, a godly nature.

While reading the scriptures in order to grow in spiritual things – in grace, faith, and power, and so on – I came across a sentence that disconcerted me the first time I read it: 'Be men!' I have never heard a man say to a horse: 'Be a horse once and for all, for I am sick of you!' You do not need to tell a horse to behave like one, because it *is* a horse and it fulfills its purpose with no difficulty; it doesn't know how to be anything but a horse. I have heard many times though: 'Be a man, because to be a man is a great accomplishment!' Why did the Holy Spirit have to inspire Paul to write such a sentence for us? Are we not people? You see, because in the Garden of Eden he lost touch with God, man gained animal instincts. Cain rose up against his brother and killed him. Lot's daughters gave their father wine to drink, and he committed incest with them because he no longer had discernment. This is what happens to the man who has no connection with God, who does not have God as the Master of his life: he loses the quality of a true man.

Darwin said that man evolved from a monkey. If monkeys could understand Darwin's theory they would condemn him, because monkeys do not kill their infants, while so many mothers today kill their babies. This is how man without God behaves! How many abortions are there today in the world? How many crimes, wars, how much hatred? This is the result of eliminating God from a man's life. Man needs to go back quickly to his Creator, the only One who can bring man back to where he was initially: near God!

Chapter 19

My dear wife and I were thanking our good God for everything He was giving us and was doing for us. We learnt from the Holy Scriptures the great and wonderful lesson of thanksgiving, according to which, if we had bread on the table, we had to thank God, knowing that so many people die of starvation every day in the world. We also learnt to thank God for the water we were drinking, because there is so much drought in some places of this world, where water is very expensive, because it is so scarce and in short supply. If we had clothes to wear we were thanking God for His care for us.

We had been married for seven years and we had no children. Mirela could not carry the pregnancy through to the end. She would get pregnant, but two months into the pregnancy, she would have a miscarriage – and she had five miscarriages in this way!

When we were without God, I had accepted that Mirela should have an abortion, and this then brought many complications to her body; so we now prayed to God and we decided to trust Him with all our hearts.

There was an opportunity to adopt a child and we were thinking that maybe this was the way God wanted to give us a child. While we were preparing the adoption papers my wife got pregnant again, so we stopped the adoption process and went to see a doctor. The doctor advised us to start some treatment, but I refused because I was afraid of possible complications, maybe repercussions, on the child. We decided to trust God for everything and our trust was fully rewarded, because after nine months, Mirela gave birth to a handsome boy that we named Daniel Ionut. After three years, God blessed us with another boy, Ioan Cosmin. Even though we would have liked to have more children, after Cosmin, my wife could not give birth to another child. We thanked God with all our hearts for the two precious gifts He gave us.

In Psalm 37 there is a verse that came true for us: *'Commit your way to the LORD; trust in him and he will do this* (Psalm 37:5).' God worked in our lives with signs and wonders. We have seen these with our own eyes; we experienced them and our hearts exalted God.

In 1997 I met a wonderful man of God in the church in Galați, a man who had a significant influence on my life of faith – Professor Ioan Panican.

I had heard that he had learnt the way of faith under the beloved Richard Wurmbrand, and Professor Ioan Panican shared with me many precious teachings and important advice; God had brought this special man to watch over my life of faith.

The worldly systems in which we live give people all sorts of methods which promise to bring happiness. For many years I thought that man's happiness is found in money, and I thought this way because I was spiritually blind. After I read the Bible, the Word of God, and after the Holy Spirit gave me the new birth, I discovered that man's happiness is found only in God, and He has given us only one blessed name: Jesus Christ. If you connect your entire life to Him, you become a happy, fulfilled and blessed man.

In Psalm 34 we find what to do in order to become truly happy: *'Whoever of you loves life and desires to see many good days, keep your tongue from evil and your lips from telling lies. Turn from evil and do good; seek peace and pursue it* (Psalm 34:12-14).' Any man who has applied the teachings of the scriptures to his life has become a blessed man.

Dear reader, maybe you have searched for happiness, peace and fulfillment for many years. How wonderful it is that God has made it possible for you to read this book! Do not stop here; seek for the most important Book on earth, the Holy Scriptures – and in it you will discover God's plan for your life. Read it, believe it and fulfil it! You will become a happy man and your family will be a blessed family. How beautiful it is when, in a family, the husband loves his wife and the wife respects and loves her husband! How wonderful it is, in a family, that the children are convinced their father loves their mother and their mother respects their father! It's like a piece of heaven that God can deposit in your family! Maybe right now, when you are reading these lines, your family is about to break up. Do not think too much! Run to God, repent of your sins and believe with all your heart in Jesus, the Son of God. The man who trusts God receives four blessings as a gift: *his sins are forgiven, his soul is saved, he becomes a child of God and he receives the gift of eternal life*. Do you think that there is someone who can give more than what God has given and still gives? No, no one ever!

Maybe you are in prison and reading this book. Do not despair! The devil who got you there tells you that there is no chance left, that everything is over, and that your life has no meaning whatsoever. My dear reader, do not believe Satan; he is the father of lies. Find a Bible, or if you have one, start reading it carefully and prayerfully. Open your heart to God. Shout to the Lord and He will not be late to answer. God, who created the heavens and the earth, loves us! It's the devil that deceives people. He even tempted the Son of God, telling Him that if He worshipped him, he would give Him all the power and glory of the kingdoms of this world. The Lord overcame the evil one saying: *'For it is written: Worship the Lord your God, and serve him only* (Matthew 4:10).' Only God is worthy and we should bring Him all worship, adoration, and praise!

So many people, fooled by the evil one, say that here on earth is both heaven and hell, but this saying is not true. This life is an exam for a man, an exam which, unfortunately, most men do not pass. Man lives a number of years on earth, years that go by so quickly! Just yesterday I was 10...then 20...then 30...and here I am over 40 years of age! Years have gone by and go by so quickly! Death comes after that, the most unwelcome guest, and then after death, there will be the judgement of God! God will judge the world according to His justice, and not how the people think they should be judged. Many people believe that through certain rituals, they can transfer the dead man's soul from one place to another, or can ease his sufferings. The Holy Scriptures, the Book that God left for us as a guide for life, does not say that. We have a parable in Luke chapter 16 which speaks of a wealthy man who died and reached the deep place of the dead, being in great torment.

Well, if he was rich, he must have left great riches behind, which his family could have used to transfer him from hell to heaven, or to ease his pains. This is not possible! If you spent your earthly life far from God, if you have not fulfilled His command, that is, to repent, then there is nothing left to be done, only a terrifying expectancy of judgement and the flames of a fire that will never be put out. So long as man is alive he needs to solve the most pressing and important problem of the soul: SALVATION. The Word of God says that Jesus Christ, who went up to heaven over two thousand years ago, will come back to judge mankind. How many people still believe this truth? So many people, in their everyday lives, prove that they do not believe what the Bible says. In Noah's time people drank, ate, got married...and they did so until the day Noah entered the Ark. After that, all of them perished in the flood that God sent because of their unbelief! In our days things are the same – in the Gospel of Matthew it is written: *'As it was in the days of Noah, so it will be at the coming of the Son of Man'* (Matthew 24:37).

I see the young people today whose parents are not concerned enough about them to direct their hearts to God. Their lives are meaningless, they have no consistency, colour or charm...I have met so many young people like this in the penitentiaries where I go to preach the gospel! If they had a bad start at such a young age, what will happen to them later?

Maybe some will try to restore themselves to society;

it's just that society offers them few chances. If you have the stigma of being a convict, then people around you will avoid you and will not desire your company. Society throws evildoers in prison, but the big mistake is the fact that they do not do anything with them there, and especially after they finish their time in prison.

In the past, I was interested only in my own self. I wanted to become someone and do something big with my life and I was living life based on the slogan 'The end justifies the means'. I thought that only murder is a great sin, but that the rest of the sins I was committing did not count, because my life was in my own hands, or so I thought. Since I entrusted my life to God, and I placed it in the hands of the One who willingly stretched them out on the cross, my life has received meaning, delight and direction. If, before, my life was only oriented towards sin, now my life is oriented only towards God, Whom I want to serve and Whom I want to please my whole life.

Maybe someone will ask: 'Are you trying to say that you sin no more?' I wish I did no longer sin, but when it happens, I know that this sin is an accident in my life. It's like when you are dressed in a white gown which you try to keep clean, avoiding everything that is filthy… there will be times when, because of carelessness or lack of watchfulness, I will stain my gown. But, when this happens, I run immediately to the One who can cleanse me, because the blood of Jesus can cleanse any confessed sin, if we regret it and leave it behind us. No one should think that you can sin anyhow and anyway you want, simply because the blood of Jesus cleanses you infinitely. Jesus forgives you, for He is good, but not if you continue to sin again and again! In the life of the believer, sin is to be an accident; it is not to be done carelessly.

The purpose God has with the believer is to make him like His Son. This is what we find in Romans 8:29: *'For those God foreknew he also predestined to be conformed to the image of his Son, that he might be the firstborn among many brothers and sisters.'* By the power of the Holy Spirit, God wants to shape us into the image of His Son. Is that possible? The Holy Scriptures, the only infallible book, say yes. At the base of this great plan that God has for each man on earth who will accept it lies OBEDIENCE to his Word.

It is great not to lie, steal, commit adultery or do anything that God does not like, and is bad for you. In Matthew 1:21, the scripture says that the Lord Jesus will save the people from their sins. What does it mean, 'will save'? It means that the Lord will release His people from their sins. This is one of the great purposes for which Jesus Christ came to earth. At the end of the Gospel of Matthew, chapter 28, our Saviour Jesus said bluntly that all power has been given to Him both in heaven and on earth. What does that mean? It means that, if you are the slave of sexual addictions, He – who has all power – can save you, can release you from these addictions. He can save you; He can release you of any vice and from any sin that enslaves you. In order for this to happen, you need to obey Him, to trust in Him. It is both wonderful and extraordinary to obey God every moment of your life! This will bring you much joy, peace, happiness and fulfilment.

People make the way of faith so complicated with all

kinds of teaching that they add to the Word of God. Jesus Christ condensed into one phrase what it means to be a true Christian: *'That which you want people to do for you, you do the same!'* How simple and how complicated at the same time! Only God can help you do to others what you would have them do to you. Imagine how beautifully we would live if we lived according to the words of the Saviour.

If Romania needs something, then that something is called FAITH IN GOD. I do not want to upset or offend anyone, but I must say this truth: most people in our nation honour God with their lips, while their life is so far from God. The Lord Jesus said: *'Not everyone who says to me, "Lord, Lord," will enter the kingdom of heaven, but only the one who does the will of my Father who is in heaven'* (Matthew 7:21). When people humble themselves, when they admit to and weep for their sins, when they pray wholeheartedly to God, and when they shun their evil ways and seek His face, He will listen from heaven, forgive their sins, and bless their country.

May God bless Romania!

Chapter 20

In the spring of 2009, God provided for me to visit the community of Romanian believers in Belgium, and I shared with a family of believers the wonderful way in which God had saved my soul.

Sharing with them about the man that the German police had mistakenly imprisoned, thinking he was a thief, and who shared the gospel with me in prison in Germany, I noticed that those around became very attentive. When I told them that this man's name was Sabău Gheorghe, and that he was from Târgoviște, one of them made a phone call and spoke with another man. After a while, other believers from Charleroi were coming. I was so amazed, and happy, to see that one of the men who got out of the car was Sabău Gheorghe – Uncle Gigi! I was so happy to see him again after fifteen years, the man whom God used in such a wonderful way in that prison in Braunschweig. I could hardly believe my eyes! The same face, the same voice, the same man who had shared the Word of God and had given me such precious advice. We were overwhelmed with emotion, and we offered heartfelt prayers of thanksgiving to God.

Sunday evening we went together to Brussels, to the Elim church, and I had the privilege and joy of sharing my testimony of how I had turned to God. Gheorghe

Sabău was in the audience without anyone knowing it. At the end of my testimony, I said that the one who had shared the gospel with me fifteen years before was in the congregation. When I said his name, Dorin Albuţ, the pastor of the Elim church, who was with me in the pulpit, had tears in his eyes; he also knew him. He invited Gigi Sabău to come to the pulpit. That was an evening when God made His presence so felt among the believers, and several souls came forward and declared that they wanted to follow the Lord Jesus. That was a night like heaven on earth! If here, on earth, we can have such moments of great joy, I wonder what it will be like when we meet the King of Kings, and see all our dear ones who have left for the Heavenly Kingdom a little earlier than us?!

One Sunday I was in Forest in Brussels, in another church of Romanians. This time Gigi Sabău was not with me, and after I shared my testimony of how God had worked in my life, I saw many tears in the eyes of those present in the church. At the end of the service, one of the believers approached me and asked me if I knew him. I said I did not. This believer was crying, and I was so amazed by what he shared with me. Fifteen years before, he had been a rebellious young man who ran away from home to look for happiness in Germany, even though he was born in a family of evangelical believers. When he reached Germany he started stealing, and one night, he robbed a shop and stole as much as he could from the things he found there. Because the police were after him, when he reached the building where he was staying, he hid the stolen goods in the room of a believer who also lived there. After that he ran and hid in a tree, not far from the room of the believer. Meanwhile, when the man arrived home, he was arrested and taken to the police department. Florin, this believer from Rădăuți, saw the entire scene from the tree. Who was the man wrongly arrested? Gigi Sabău. I could hardly believe that, after 15 years, I found out the truth in Forest, Brussels.

I asked Florin to meet with Gigi Sabău the next day, and he agreed. After 15 years Gheorghe Sabău found out the truth of why he had been imprisoned.

What a great God we have! If God sent Joseph to prison to save an entire people, the Israelites, God also allowed Gigi Sabău to be unjustly imprisoned so that He could save Vasile Tofan and make him one of His children. Blessed be our God for the riches of His grace, poured out on the entire world.

I strongly pray to God that all those who read this story of a man who looked for the glory and riches of this world, but to whom God gave the new birth in such unusual circumstances, would seriously ask these questions: Who am I? Where do I come from? Where am I going? May my readers get hold of a Bible and read it, and then ask for power from God to fulfil it.

The Bible is the only book where man can find answers to these questions. Religion, no matter what it is like or what it is called, cannot save anyone. The Apostle Peter, in Acts 4:12, says: *'Salvation is found in no one else, for there is no other name under heaven given to mankind by which we must be saved.'* This name that Peter is talking about is Jesus Christ, the Name above all Names, because it belongs to the Son of God. That which is written in the Holy Scriptures is true, it has come true, it is coming true and will come true. If it says that Jesus will return in the clouds from heaven, this will come true, no doubt about it!

I pray for all those who will read these lines, that God, who gave me the grace to write, may bless them too. Those who have made the decision to follow the Lord Jesus Christ for all their life should get closer and closer to Him and so be sanctified more and more. May God help us to live our lives according to His will, every day that He gives to us.

Maybe you have read these lines and you are a defeated Christian, or maybe you have left the House of God for no reason; or maybe you feel downcast, slammed… In the Name of Lord Jesus, please stand up, shake yourself and remember the prodigal son; then go back to God, who never tires of forgiving you. Shut your ears to the whispers of the evil one, who is telling you that, for you, everything is finished. Be strengthened, be a man of courage and go forward to heaven, holding tight to the Author and Perfecter of our faith, Jesus Christ.

I wish, and I pray to God, to be able to go to as many prisons as possible in the country where I was born, to tell the people there about the extraordinary pardon 'decree' that God has given: the gospel of our Lord Jesus. This decree can truly make you a free man! In the Epistle of the Apostle Paul to the Romans it is written that the gospel of Christ is the power of God for the salvation, for the deliverance of everyone who believes. There can be a decree by the president of the country and you can be free in one day, escaping the punishment you would have had to go through; but if you are not a born-again man, sooner or later, you will end up in prison again. Maybe you are already there for the second, third or umpteenth time. The president's decree cannot help you too much, but the decree God has given can free you from the prison of sin which ruins your life, and by which, if you do not get out, you will be forever condemned by the justice of God.

May these lines help you understand that the Lord Jesus Christ died for you too. He has risen and now sits at the right hand of God. If you believe in Him, He will intercede for you, so that you need no longer live for yourself, but for Him, the One who died and rose again, Jesus the Redeemer!

I pray that God would bless Romania, Israel, His chosen people, and the whole world. Amen!

Vasile and his wife Mirela live in the southeastern part of Romania

They have two sons, Daniel and Cosmin